The Spirit of Sixteen

Written and Illustrated by
M. Ann Machen Pritchard

MAMP Creations

952-938-9320

www.mampcreations.com

©2022 By M. Ann Machen Pritchard

All Rights Reserved

Editor: Sequoya Nelson

ISBN-13: 978-09772210-2-8

ISBN-10: 0-9772210-2-4

No part of this book may be used or reproduced in any manner whatsoever without the written permission from the publisher or author.

Printed in the United States of America.

This book is dedicated to everyone who has been through hard times in life. May this book help you to have the courage to overcome your trials and tribulations and come to know the Lord.

" I believe that with faith in God we can get through anything."

John 3:16 taken from the King James version of the Bible.

For God so loved the world, that he gave his only begotten Son, that whosoever believeth in him should not parish, but have everlasting life.

Acknowledgments

First, I would like to thank God for giving me strength and courage.

I especially, want to say thank you to my children, Sequoya and Danny, Jr. Also, my grandchildren.

You are all a joy to me.

Thank you to Dee Hobbie and the late Nancy Fish of the former Bywords Printing & Print Solutions in St. Paul, MN for believing in me.

I would like to say thank you to many family and friends who believe in me and support me. You all know who you are. There are so many that I will not list names because I know that I might miss someone.

I would like to say a special thank you to Lester Odom, Mary Lou Garza, Barbara Cole and Laurie Etchen for believing in me and supporting me.

Preface:

The Spirit of Sixteen is based on a true story. The names and places have been changed to preserve anonymity.

If anyone's name or place is similar, it is just a coincidence.

Contents

Chapter 1. Violation of Soul

Chapter 2. Afraid

Chapter 3. Withdrawn and Depressed

Chapter 4. Don't Trust Anybody

Chapter 5. Life Lessons

Chapter 6. The Kidnapping and Assault

Chapter 7. Epilogue

Chapter 8. Love & Light with Poems/Songs/Advice

Final Thoughts

Introduction

This is a story that is a chronical of moments that changed a little girl, and later a woman's life, and how faith and the promise of God's love brought Gloria Ann through many dark events in her life, primarily in her relationships. "The Spirit of Sixteen" is a saying that Gloria starts using after her first traumatic event in her life. This is based on a familiar to most verse in the Bible, John 3:16. Gloria Ann in her story goes on to show that with God nothing can keep her down and she is worthy of love.

Violation of Soul

Chapter 1

On a hot sunny day, July 1, 1953 to be exact, a bright skinned little baby girl with beautiful wavy black hair and the darkest brown eyes was born. Yes, that would be me. "How cute she is!" everyone would say. I did not enter the world in a cold hospital room, but at what would be my home in a small room with a midwife named Mrs. Kinsley. She had delivered most babies in the area, and had a smile that would light up the room. My Momma was a very lovely lady named Linda Freely, with light golden-brown skin and hair that went down her back who already had three births before me. However, one of the children, my sister named Cindy, died before she ever had a chance to have a life in this world. She was a stillborn baby.

So, I guess you can say that I am number three now of the four living children. I have an older brother named Joe, Jr. who is 13 and a younger brother named Tony who is 3. Also, I have an older sister that is 12 named Elaine. Oh, yes, I can't forget about myself, I am now age 5. But you would think that I was 5 going on 25, according to the grown folks around me... ha...ha...ha. I was very adventurous and was not afraid of anything.

We lived in Barker, Kentucky a small little country town as some may say in the South. My parents named me Gloria Ann Freely. The Freely's were a very loved and respected family in Barker. My Dad was a Baptist Minister, the Reverend Joe Freely, Sr. who lived the way God led him.

He was a very hard worker that also worked for the town's Moving Company, Mountain Movers, Inc. as a side job because being a minister did not always bring in enough money to take care of our family.

I loved to hear my momma sing to me as she rocked me in this old rocking chair. She had rocked many other little children before my siblings and I in that old chair because she used to baby sit other people's children to make extra money for the family. I don't understand what was so special about that chair. But it sure was a good old rocking chair with the most beautiful flower design on the seat cushion that my Momma would sit on. It had pink flowers with a white and blue background with this green curly vine on it. The seat cushion reminded me of a bright sunny day with a beautiful blue sky. Momma loved rocking in that chair; I think it gave her peace in the chaos of raising her own kids as well as taking care of the kids that weren't hers.

My Momma used to sing the Lullaby song to me to get me to sleep at night. Then she would hum it, "Lullaby, and good night... hum... hum." You all know that one, right? I loved snuggling up in her warm lap and my Momma's beautiful soft skin. Many people in the neighborhood said that I was sweet, cute and all of the things a mother and father would want in a child. Now I'm going to tell you a story that changed my life.

My Uncle Jesse would always say that I was his favorite. He used to bring me my favorite chocolate candy that had lots of almonds in it when he and Aunt Carol would drive from Florida to come for visits to our house. Sometimes I would be ashamed that we had to live in our house because it was old and worn down a lot. The screen door on the front had holes in it and the wooden frame needed some repairs. And yes, you guessed it, the house needed to have a new roof on it because it did leak every time that it would rain hard during a bad storm. Uncle Jesse and Aunt Carol didn't seem to care though. We always had a good time laughing and joking, and the adults would reminisce about old times when they were growing up.

I always wished that Uncle Jesse and Aunt Carol would take me to Florida with them so I could see what it felt like to live in a nice house like theirs. I had only gotten to see some pictures of their house. Their house was made of beautiful red bricks and had a nice roof. It had these green and white shutters on the windows that you would see in books. Aunt Carol planted beautiful flower bushes in the front. I especially liked the red roses that seemed to always be blooming. They had a couple of orange trees, an apple tree and some green grape vines, too. Uncle Jesse even planted a vegetable garden every year in the back. They had a lot of land! I was always so happy to see them.

One day when I knew that they were going to be coming to visit us I was so excited that I walked out of the house to sit on the front porch to wait for them. While I was sitting on the porch, swinging my skinny legs and humming to myself, I heard a noise that sounded like it was coming from this old barn near our house. I knew I was supposed to stay on the porch and wait for my Uncle Jesse and Aunt Carol, but figured I would only go off a little way and only for a minute.

Being the typical curious (aka nosey) kid, I decided to go and find out where exactly that clicking noise was coming from. Click...click...click. It was beginning to make my ears hurt. I could hear the sound getting louder and louder as I was walking down to the creek near our house. Before I knew it, I had walked too far away from our house and did not see the house anymore. The noise was coming from this old wooden barn that looked like it was about to fall apart. I got very curious, so I walked up the grassy hill to get closer to where the noisy clicking sound was coming from. When I got closer to the old worn-down barn I saw this older boy dressed in blue jeans with dirty grass stains on them and a red shirt, and he had on black tennis shoes hammering some metal inside the barn. When he saw me, he stopped, and smiled at me and asked, "Where is your brother Joe, Jr?" I answered, "I think he had gone fishing with his friend Patrick." I was a little confused because I didn't know how he knew I was Joe's sister.

He told me that his name is Greg Dopely and that he is a good friend of my brother, Joe, Jr. and that I shouldn't be wandering far from home. Then he asked me to come with him around to the other side of that old worn-down barn because he wanted to show me something he was working on, and that my brother Joe, Jr. will probably be coming there soon looking for me to take me back home. So, I trusted him and followed him to the other side of that old barn, because he told me that he was a friend of my brother.

Also, that we can wait around there for Joe, Jr. to come to get me. I got very quiet and started to get afraid.

It was very creepy around there with lots of weeds and an old rusty looking barbed wire fence. There weren't any other people, and I couldn't see my house. I'm sure Momma was wondering where I'd gone.

I did not understand why he would want me to follow him around to the back side of that old worn-down barn to wait for Joe, Jr. to come to get me, but I trusted him because he told me that he is a good friend of my brother. I began to get a lot more frightened that my legs were shaking and I felt really nervous. While we were walking, he chuckled and kept telling me to not be afraid because he was going to show me something very nice that I might like.

Much to my surprise, Greg was not a good person at all. I had thought that since he knew my brother Joe, Jr. that it would be okay to follow him. I really wanted to go back to my porch and wait for my uncle. But he was a very angry and hateful person when we got around to the back side of the old barn where no one could see us. I didn't understand what was going on. As soon as we were around the corner, he grabbed me by the throat and pulled me down to the ground and pulled my pants down. I did not know what to do and asked him not to hurt me, and asked him what he was doing. He told me that he was not going to hurt me. But he unzipped his pants. Then he took his private part of his body and touched it to mine. He asked me if it felt good. Then he kept asking me, "Does it hurt?" It hurt me so bad that I was in so much pain and shock that I could not even scream. I was quiet as the tears trickled down my face. I was in shock so I did not say a word. I did not understand what he was doing to me but I know it hurt me so bad. He was sweaty and dirty and gross. I wanted my Momma so bad.

His eyes were as red as a devil's eyes. His breath smelled like a hog swamp. After a few minutes I was able to finally kick him, pull my pants up and I ran away as fast as I could. But unfortunately, tried to go back the way I came, and I ran into the fence and it cut my right leg. I screamed when I saw the blood dripping down my leg and started shaking uncontrollably. Suddenly, he caught up with me and grabbed me by my throat with his nasty smelly hands and started choking me. Then he stopped choking me and yelled at me and said, "If you make another sound I will rip your throat out with this barbed wire fence! And if you ever tell anyone what happened here I know where to find you and you will be as dead as a dead duck." I believed him. I had never been so scared and confused. All I knew was that I wanted to be home, with my Momma in that old rocking chair and her humming to me.

I blacked out at some point. I don't know how much time had passed, but he was still there. I prayed very hard for God to save me from this bad person. I just know that when I woke up all of a sudden before he did any more damage to me I heard my sister, Elaine calling out my name," Gloria Ann…Gloria Ann… where are you?" she shouted. "Momma is going to be so mad if you don't come home!" Exasperated, she called into the air "Where did you wander off to?" I was glad someone was looking for me. I was so frightened and prayed for God to take care of me as tears continued to spill down my small face. I didn't know how to stop. I didn't know what to do; I was so paralyzed with fear. My body hurt, I felt dirty, and my leg was bleeding. I just wanted to be home. That monster of a boy finally let me go when he heard Elaine calling for me, but not without one last warning to keep my mouth shut.

I ran out from the back of that old worn-down barn and Greg hid in some weeds so he could not be seen. I saw Elaine and ran as quickly as I could to her, crying the whole way. When I finally got to her, she asked me, "What is wrong with you?" I told her that I ran into the barbed wire fence and cut my leg.

I asked her, "Do you believe in the spirit of sixteen?" But she did not answer me, nor did she probably even understood what I meant by that. She just looked at my leg and said that she would clean it up, put a Band-Aid on it and that it will feel better. She gave me a hug and told me that she was sorry that I cut my leg. I love my sister. Then Elaine took me home and I went into the house with her but never said a word to her about what actually happened to me. She put me in the tub because I was all dirty. She said, "You must have fallen down because your clothes are filthy. Were you rolling in the field? "She told me to never wonder off again because something could happen to me. But what she didn't know is that something did happen to me. I was attacked by one of my brother's friends. I just sniffled, and changed my clothes, nodded and said I wouldn't do it again. She had no idea how sorry I really was.

The boy named Greg, scared and hurt me so bad that I promised him that I would never tell anyone what he did to me because I was afraid that he could come back after me like he said that he would. I would be as dead as a dead duck according to him, and I sure did believe him. But I did try to tell my Momma once. I was so scared and did not talk very loud so she must not have heard what I wanted to say because she was so busy keeping up with my little brother, Tony and house chores that she was trying to get done. She never looked up, and when she asked if I was trying to say something, I clammed up and shook my head. At that moment I felt so lost and afraid. I never wanted to speak again. I became very shy and just stayed very quiet at home, at school and everywhere. I felt that I could not trust anyone. I thought that I was not good enough for anything. I had nightmares thinking that someone was going to grab me from underneath my bed at night. Some nights I wouldn't even sleep because I was so scared that my nightmares would come true. As time went on, whenever any of my brother, Joe, Jr.'s friends would come to our house to hang out with him and make remarks about how pretty I was I would feel really ugly and dirty. I made sure that I was not left alone with any of them. I didn't know if they were all mean like his friend Greg or not. I didn't want to be touched like that ever again. I was so confused. Even if any of the grown up family friends or relatives would say that I was so cute or that I was so pretty and that I was going to be so beautiful when I grow up it would make me sick to my stomach.

After a while I started having dreams about a man that was with these two beautiful women, one on each side of him and they were calling me to come with them. I was afraid and would not go with them because they were not like normal people because they did not walk on the floor. It was as if they were just floating in the air towards the ceiling in my little bedroom. "Come join us", they said. I would reply, "No. I am just going to stay down here." I didn't know why I kept having the same dream or what it meant, but when I woke up after the third time of having the same dream I just blocked out everything that had happened to me about the attack. But I did remember that someone had hurt me. I just did not remember the details of what happened anymore after those dreams.

A year went by, and it was time for me to go to school and I was afraid to go. I had become so shy around people, especially strangers I did not know—whether or not if it was a kid or an adult. I remember the first day of 1st grade in school all of the Moms would bring their kids to the classroom. When my Mom brought me to the class I was so afraid for her to leave me and I cried. I kept holding on to her and did not want to let go. I was afraid that I would not know what to do at school. After a few days I did not cry anymore when I went to school, and began to relax. I had made some new friends and things were beginning to be fun for me. Play time and writing were my favorite parts of the school day. Even though I had some friends, one thing I didn't like at school was snack time. Remember, my family was very poor and could not afford to buy me any snacks to take to school like what the other kids had. I remember one day I finally did bring in something to eat at snack time but it was not a good snack at all. It was a piece of toasted bread and I put some homemade grape jelly on it but when I took it out of my lunch bag it was all messed up and soggy. Most of the kids in class laughed at me. I told them that it was good. I was so embarrassed that I never wanted to bring in a snack again.

In my class, there was one kind little boy named T.J. that had brought in a bag of store-bought potato chips for his snack time. He offered to share his snack with me. He was one of the nicest kids at school.

My family did not live far from the school so I did not mind walking, unless it was raining. I would hate it when it would rain the night before because I could not get enough sleep from the beating of the raindrops hitting our roof like a drum.

The roof on our house needed to be repaired but my Dad could not afford to get it fixed yet. So, every time that the hard rain came down our roof would leak really badly, especially in my bedroom. I remember my brother Joe, Jr. bringing two large buckets into my room and setting them down where the water would be dripping down onto my bed. I had to try to sleep the best that I could. I would stay awake for most of the night because I would hear the water leaking down into the buckets.... drip...drip...drip. When it would rain harder the roof would leak even more...drip...drip...drip. The rain would come down faster and harder. Sometimes it would be so cold that I would shiver and have to get another blanket put on my bed in the dry corner I curled up in. I pray for God to let this rain stop. Please God stop the rain, and let Daddy get enough money for a new roof!

Even though my family had some hard times I was thankful to at least have a place to sleep despite the conditions. There were times that I thought that the roof was going to cave in on me. The mattress that I had to sleep on was so old and worn out the springs would sometimes pop up and I would get a cut on my leg or arm from the sharp end of the springs. That was not fun at all, and full of lumps, so it was impossible to get comfortable. I dreamed of the day that I could get a new roof and a new bed. I often wondered why I was even born into this family. Was this God's plan for me to have to live like this? I would remember my Aunt Carol and Uncle Jesse's house and wish I could live in a place like theirs. Or, maybe they could come and take me to live with them. But, then I would miss my Momma and Daddy, and my brothers and sister like crazy, so I guess I was stuck.

We hardly had food to eat sometimes Whenever I had a birthday, I don't remember ever having a real birthday party. I remember being invited to my friends' parties, but was never allowed to go to any of them except for one because my Momma and Dad could not afford to buy a birthday gift for the children.

One year, I decided to change that! On my 8th birthday, I decided to just throw myself a birthday party and invite all of my friends from school…without telling my Momma! So, I invited my entire 2nd grade class to come to my house after school to my birthday party. Of course, I told them to not bring me any gifts because all I want is for my friends to come and celebrate my birthday with me and play and have lots of fun. Wow! We had so much fun just playing games together. My Momma was surprised to see these kids at the house, but I told her we would just play outside and we had fun anyway. My favorite game was hide and seek. We all played until the sun went down. Then all of my friends left except for one, my friend Lisa.

Lisa's Mom came walking fast down the street to our house and asked,

"Hey Linda, is the party over yet?"

My Momma answered,
"What party? There was no party here. All there was were a lot of kids playing here with Gloria Ann all day."

Lisa's Mom, Mrs. Lane told Lisa to get home right away before she gets a good whooping. I told Mrs. Lane to please don't whoop Lisa, because we were just having too much fun playing that we forgot about what time it was. I never did tell my Momma that I had invited my whole school class over for my birthday party. I just let her believe that the kids just came over to our house to play with me. But that was the best birthday that I had ever had. It meant so much to me to just have fun playing with my friends from school to celebrate my birthday.

I did not have any birthday gifts or balloons like my friends told me that they had gotten on their birthdays, but the fun times that I had playing with my friends was my birthday gift. I don't understand why some kids mostly care about how many or what gifts they get on their birthday. What is the most special gift to me is to have lots of fun playing with my friends. Because I never had five kids come to my house to play all at one time before.

Afraid

Chapter 2

When I was in 1st grade our school had built a new very large sliding board. It was so shiny and looked very slick; which meant you could go really fast. Everyone was so excited and couldn't wait for their turn to try it out. When it was my turn to climb up the very tall steps to go up, I was hesitant. I was afraid of heights so I was nervous and didn't really want a turn, but the teacher and the other children pressured me to climb up and to not be so scared. They assured me that this would be a fun thing to do during recess, and all I had to do is to slide down the sliding board. I didn't want anyone making fun of me for being scared, so I began to climb the skinny metal stairs.

Once I got to the top I panicked and would not move because I did not want to slide down. One of the boys that were behind me was impatient, and he pushed me down and I made a very fast descent down the slick metal. I slid down half way and fell off and landed hard on the ground. I hit my nose and it was bleeding profusely. The teacher, Mrs. Colleen, rushed over in a full-on panic and asked one of the students to run and get help inside of the school. But my nose was bleeding so bad that when she saw one of the girls that had a large handkerchief that was already torn, she ripped off a section of it to help to put some pressure on my nose to try to stop the bleeding. I was so scared. Eventually, it stopped and I was able to go home. All I wanted was my Momma. When I got home I lay down and slept for the rest of the day until the next morning.

I cried elephant tears when I woke up because I saw big bruises on my nose and face when I looked at myself into the mirror in the bathroom. I thought that I looked like the ugliest person in the whole entire school now. I did not even want to go back to school ever again.

I finally got healed up after several weeks. I think I probably had broken my nose but back in those days black folks were not allowed to be seen in the local hospital in most places in the South. If we needed medical attention a doctor would need to come to our house. But since I could still function, I guess everyone thought that I would be okay. That was the mentality in those days. No doctors unless it was a matter of life and death. I actually was okay, so there was no need to see a doctor, thank goodness. I was so glad because I don't like needles! When I think of a doctor I think of the big needles that they use to give shots. I definitely did not want to be taking any shots!

After being bullied to slide down that giant sliding board I was not sure if I wanted to play on the playground again because if the other children like pushing children around that were afraid, then maybe I should not go to school anymore.

But, I of course kept going to school. My Momma thought that was not a good enough reason (or any reason was good for that matter). Another incident that happened later in school was that the children in the class were playing around by going in and out of the lockers in our class. I thought that it would be fun to join them and also not feel out of place. But low and behold was that a big mistake. After about five minutes one of my classmates locked the door of the locker that I was in and laughed at me. He ran away from the locker quickly like a bolt of lightning. I was so afraid because it was dark inside there. I panicked and yelled as loud as I could for someone to let me out.

"Let me out of here!" I cried out. "Let me out of heeeerrree!"

I began to pound on the door and screamed,

"Let me out of here. It is dark in here! I can't breathe!"

It was also very hot inside of the locker. The sweat was running down my face. My eyes were burning as if they were on fire, and so were my lungs, because I felt like each breath was being squeezed out of me. I was panicking even more. I pounded so hard and rocked the locker (as it was not attached to the wall), and it finally toppled over and fell onto the floor. I got super scared then and that thump over made my body hurt, too. I just stayed quiet because I did not know what was happening outside of the dark locker as I could not see anything.

Suddenly, I heard two custodians rushing into the room to raise up the locker from the floor. I could tell that there were two of them because I could hear two sets of boots clanking heavily as they made their way down the hall to the classroom.

Apparently, the teacher, Mrs. Colleen, must have called them to come and help. Thank goodness! I didn't think I could take another minute of being closed up in that steamy locker like a caterpillar in a cocoon. Once the custodians put the locker upright and opened the door for me to come out my knees were like jello and so shaky because I was still so afraid. The teacher asked the other children who was the one that locked me into the locker but no one answered her. So, she punished the whole class by having them to write 100 times, "I will not lock any of my classmates into a locker ever again."

Most of the class was very angry that the kid that actually locked me in the locker did not confess. I am so afraid of the dark now that I get really scared at night and want to leave a hall light on so I can see in case I need to get up to go to the bathroom or maybe to the kitchen to get some water. But, my parents aren't having any of that. They always want all of the lights off in the house once everyone is in the bed to go to sleep. They didn't believe in "wasting" electricity, as folks say.

I had nightmares for several nights following that incident. I don't believe that I could completely get over the trauma of being in the dark in that locker. I thank God that my parents finally allowed me to at least leave the hall light on at night so I would not be as afraid once they saw that I was really having a hard time.

Withdrawn and Depressed

Chapter 3

By the time that I was nine years old I became withdrawn and depressed. I was not at all like the original care-free bright-eyed little girl that my family was used to seeing, but yet no one did anything to help either. I was further upset again one day at school because most of my friends were playing games on teams. The teams were all filled up so I did not have a team to play on. So, I just put my head down, dejected, and sat in a corner of the gym. After a few minutes a couple of my friends Julie and Terri came over to talk to me to try to get me to play on a new team that they wanted to start because that way all three of us could play on the same team.

I began to feel a little bit better but I still thought that someone should have picked me to be on a team at first along with the other kids. No one ever likes to feel left out.

When school was over for the day, I went home walked quietly and timidly into the kitchen like I always did after school. I sat on the old beat up looking stool near the table that my Mom was always at. She was making some homemade loaves of plain white bread. The kitchen smelled like yeast, and normally I would have been excited because she made the best homemade bread. I watched her as she was kneading the dough, then said,

"Mom, I feel like no one loves me or cares about me at all."

"Why do you feel that way, Gloria Ann?" she asked.

"Because I had no one to pick me to play a game on a team when the other kids were all picked. I felt really left out."

"Finally, after all of the other kids were picked to play I just went over to the corner and just sat down."

"I felt really bad that no one wanted me to be on their team. "

"I think that I know why though. I know I am not as athletic as the other kids. I am smaller than everyone else so my legs just cannot keep up when it is time to run and jump really fast."

My Mom said,

"I love you and care about you, so does your Dad along with your sister Elaine, your brothers, Joe, Jr. and Tony. "

"Also, always remember that God loves you. "

"I guess I had not thought about it that way before." I replied to my Mom in a tearful voice as tears threatened to start falling. I thought to myself "Don't start crying, girl. Once you start you won't be able to stop."

"So, with my wonderful family and God to love me and be my friend I always have a friend?" I asked with quivering lips.

"Yes." Mom answered.

"But I thought that I still need the kids at school to love, care about me, and be my friends." Holding back my tears. I was sniffling at this point, and wiped my big dark brown eyes.

My Mom said,

"All of the kids at school don't have to be your friend. When you have one or two good friends that is all of the friends that you need. "That is enough friends to have. Your family will also always be there."

"OK."

"So now I know that Julie and Terri must be my good friends because they are the only two kids that came to ask me to be on the new team that they wanted to make so I could also play on a team."

"I love you, Gloria Ann." Mom said while smiling like she had just opened a big present.

Smiling back at her with no tears in my eyes anymore,

"I love you, too, Mom."

After I thought about it I walked into the living room and took the Bible off of the coffee table and began to look for the bible verse that I love so much, John 3:16. (From the Bible, King James version).

For God so loved the world that he gave his only begotten son that whosoever believeth in him should not parish but have everlasting life.

That made me feel better, and I tried to not let it bother me anymore if I wasn't picked to be with everyone else.

Don't Trust Anybody

Chapter 4

Well, it is going on 6:00 pm and the Choir Director of our youth choir had not arrived for rehearsal yet. Where could she be? There are several preteens at the church waiting and they were getting very impatient. They don't know what to do so they decided that they wanted to play a game or something. What three of them decided to do was very wrong and frightening. I could not believe what they were doing. "God forbid these kids! Help me Lord!" "What is wrong with these kids?"

They were trying the do the most ungodly things to other kids. When I tried to stop them, they decided that I was next. Two of them who were girls grabbed me by my legs and arms, the third one; a boy took a mop handle and tried to shove it up my private parts! "Stop!

Stop, I cried. This is not a game." I was so afraid and was crying so hard. They finally stopped and began to laugh at me and told me that they were not really going to do anything to me but they wanted to just scare me a little bit. I told them that God will punish them for what they did. Even though they did not put the mop handle up my private parts it was a very frightening thing to experience. Especially for someone to do such evil things inside of the church. It was disgusting. Oh, my goodness, I cannot trust anybody. But I do trust God. God is the only one that I can ever trust now, I thought. Just like my Momma told me.

The Choir Director finally arrived for choir rehearsal and we went on with the rehearsal. None of us kids mentioned anything about what had happened to us. We just let it go and went on with the rehearsal as though nothing had happened because we knew that the Choir Director would probably not believe us. Because we were young people, we did not believe that any adults would believe anything that we would say because we were taught to listen and not ever talk about anything back in those days. Children did not really have a voice back then. I always loved to go to church because that was the safest place that I found peace. But on that day, I began to rethink things. What had always been a place of comfort, solace, and feeling free no longer felt that way after those terrible older kids.

I remember back when I joined the church and gave my life to Christ at the young age of 9 years old. When I heard this one song that touched my soul I felt this tingly happy chill like feeling that everything was going to be alright.

Remember all of the stuff that I told you about earlier? I felt that God saved me from being killed or hurt worse than I was when I was younger and thought that giving my life to Christ would save my soul from everything bad. I felt that God had saved me again on the day of that choir rehearsal with those mean kids.

I don't know why people want to hurt people. It's just not right. I never did anything to hurt anyone so why should anyone want to hurt me? I just don't understand. I just could not comprehend how people can be so cruel. My brother's friend, kids at school, and now these awful older kids at my own church. I put all of my faith in God that he would always protect me.

Again, my favorite Bible verse John 3:16 popped into my head.

For God so loved the world that he gave his only begotten son that whosoever believeth in him should not parish but have everlasting life.

I carried that verse in my head with me everywhere for many years, and the Spirit of Sixteen is what carried me through. I figured if God loved me, he will always be with me and protect me. With faith in God we can get through anything, even when things aren't always great.

Life Lessons

Chapter 5

As the years went by I mostly stayed to myself and did not talk much to anyone. I thought it was better to just go to school and read books. I did not even go to any of the ballgames when I was in high school except for my senior year. Going to the basketball games were fun because they were inside the gym where it was nice and warm (remember we were pretty poor and my house wasn't always warm). But I did not like to go to the football games much at all because they were outside and sometimes it got very cold. I hated the cold, but I went anyway. I thought that my toes would fall right off if I was not careful because of the cold weather. The next football game I took a blanket with me to try to stay warm. But, even that did not help much when it was a colder night. So after about a couple of football games I quit going.

I did not really know what was going on anyway. Just these boys running and some of them would get tackled to the ground. Some would even get hurt like a broken leg or a sprained ankle. I think one kid broke his collar bone. I decided that I had enough of football for a while!

In high school I was so excited to get my first job at this clothing store. I had so many cool clothes. I spent most of the money that I made on new clothes and shoes for the first few months of working. We didn't have a lot of money, so we didn't really have nice things, and had to do without a lot of things that a lot of the other kids had. But then I decided that I had to start saving money to buy my own car so my Dad would not have to keep taking me to work every day. Life definitely seemed to start getting easier for me after all the tough moments when I was younger.

My dad worked long hours at the moving company he worked for. I am sure that it was a little hard on my Dad sometimes having to get up from sitting in his recliner chair after just having a few minutes to rest from working hard all day. But he always smiled and drove me to work and got me there on time. I loved and appreciated my Dad so much. He never complained about driving me.

"Gloria Ann one of these days you are going to buy your own car and you can take me to work, ha…ha…ha, "he would say and chuckle.

"But seriously, I am so proud of you. You are doing so good getting a good job and learning how to save money to buy your own car someday."

"I can see it now." Dad whispered in my ear so Mom would not hear him. Because she did not think that I should go in debt to have car payments just yet.

He insisted that the time will come sooner than I would think, and have faith that it would happen.

I eventually graduated from high school, and it took me a whole year to save up fourteen hundred dollars to put a down payment on a car. Wow, I thought that I was rich! I did not think that I would save that much money. Dad and I went looking for my new car a couple of weeks later. Well, it probably will not be spanking brand new but it will be new to me.

We looked and looked for several days but I could not make up my mind on what kind of car that I would like to have. I like the more sporty looking cars but my Dad kept showing me these older looking kinds of cars that older people buy. Frustrated, he finally told me that maybe I should ask my brother Joe, Jr. to help me look for a car that I would like that I would be able to afford.

So, about a week later my brother Joe, Jr. took me car shopping. Wow, was that a lot of fun. I loved hanging out with my big brother, and it made me feel good that he wanted to hang out and help his little sister. Joe, Jr. drove me from one lot to the next. I still could not make up my mind. But then once we were finally getting tired of looking I saw this little car that was just staring at me to buy it. It was a 1969 Chevy Camaro. The color was a beautiful shiny royal blue with black interior. It had sparkling chrome wheels the best car that I have ever seen. It definitely wasn't new, but it sure was nice. Wow! I have to buy this car, I thought to myself. This is the one!

I did not even test drive the car because I was afraid to. I still had a lot of anxiety, and I loved the car, but was scared to drive. I asked Joe, Jr. to test drive it for me. He went into the Barker's Used Cars dealership to get a salesman to come to help us.

As soon as Joe, Jr. got the keys to the car he got in and told me to get into the passenger's side because we were going to take this baby for a ride.

Well we went for a ride alright. Joe, Jr. loved the car so much he told me that we have to go and find our younger brother Tony to bring him out for a ride. But what happened instead was he drove home to pick Tony up, but told me to just stay home for a few minutes and they will come back to get me.

Joe, Jr. started to laugh and said,

"Hey, Gloria Ann we will see you later. We want to go on the bigger highway to really blow this car out to see how fast it can go." "Because if it doesn't run well on the highway then it will not be a good car for you."

Joe, Jr. and Tony took the car to I don't know where and were gone for about forty-five minutes.

When my brothers finally came back to pick me up to take me back to the dealership to put a hold deposit on the car it was almost time for it to close. Thank goodness! We got there just in time to put the one-hundred-dollar deposit down to hold it until the next day so I can go to the bank to get a loan to go with the $1,400.00 that I had saved.

The next day, Friday morning May 20th, 1972 I woke up early at 7:00 a.m. My Dad was off work so he could take me downtown to the Press Bank to get a loan so I can pay a down payment and get my car payments set up. Since this is my first time buying a car I made sure that my Dad could be my co-signer.

Dad and I went to the bank and I told the loan officer, Mr. Banner that I plan to put $1,300.00 down on the car. Also, that I needed to get a loan for the balance of $1,200.00 because the cost of the car is $2,500.00. I told him my Dad has good credit so he can be my co-signer for the loan.

Mr. Banner looked at me and had this funny grin on his face and said,

"Wow!

"Since you are paying that much money for your down payment then you don't even need to have a Co-signer, young lady."

"You are paying down more money than the loan is for so the bank is ok for you not to need a co-signer. "

"You can get the car loan on your own with just your name on it."

Mr. Banner told me that I was doing well because a lot of kids out here buying cars usually had to have one of their parents to co-sign for them. I was so proud of myself! After I signed the paperwork for the loan and talked to an insurance agent to make sure that I had the car insured my Dad drove me to the dealership to pay for the car and pick it up.

Once we got back home from getting the car my brothers Joe, Jr. and Tony came running out the door saying that they need me to drive them to go pick up a friend and to get some things at the store. I told them that they can just drive it because I was too afraid to drive too far anywhere yet.

To my surprise my brothers were gone with my car for about three hours. I did not know that they would be gone that long. It had gotten dark outside now and I won't get to go to where I need to go because I have not driven a car at night time before.

When my Dad heard me say that I was afraid to drive my car he told me that I can't just have my brothers driving me around because the car is mine and I have to learn how to drive it. So, he asked me to drive him to the grocery store so he can get some more apples because Mom was going to make an apple pie tomorrow.

So, I slowly got into my car and Dad handed me the keys. There was a silence for about a couple of minutes. He was waiting for me to set my mirrors and whatever else that I needed to do. I was still just sitting there after setting the mirrors. Dad said,

"What are we waiting for?" You must turn on the head lights."

I said to him, "I have no idea where the light switch is Dad."

He said,

"You need to look on the dashboard for it and you will find it."

"Oh, okay!"

Just a simple thing as turning on the lights of my car made me a little nervous at first because I had never had my own car before, and not really driven very much. It was taking me a little time to get used to it. But once I got the hang of where all of the light switches and locks, etc. were I was ready to drive my Dad to the grocery store that night. I put the car in gear, slowly reversed out of the driveway, and away we went.

After I drove Dad back home from the grocery store, he decided that I needed to drive him to the hardware store to pick up a couple of pairs of work gloves that he needed.

I believe that he did that so I could get more used to driving my car. You know how things go, practice, practice, practice. The more places that I drive around the more used to and comfortable I will be, or at least that's what he said. I was really getting good at driving after I got through that first night. My Dad always encouraged me to be the best that I can be in anything that I want to do.

In about a week and a half I was driving everywhere. I thought that I was something else now in my "new" car that was not really new because it was four years old.

I was even picking up some of my co-workers on my way to go to work. Eventually, I was going out to hang out with some of my friends in town when we got off for the evening.

About four months had passed and I was really good at driving and playing the radio loud like the other teenagers were doing back then. The next thing that I knew some of the kids would stop at the red light and challenge me to drag race with them. And guess what? Yes, I made a bad choice of accepting their challenge so I would race them down the road to the next red light.

But after a few races I decided that it was not a good idea at all because someone could have gotten into an accident or something bad could have happened. Then one night someone tried to run me clear off the road because he was drunk.

I knew that God must have been watching over me for sure. I was so scared that I told myself that I better not be doing anymore racing down the road.

There was not much to do for teenagers back then, especially in a small town, so what else could we get into? Well, all we basically did was just drive up and down the road, then turn into the local hamburger joint to see who was there, then out the parking lot and down the road again. But that can be very boring after a while.

I decided to travel to different churches with my Dad so I can see other places. But one time I remember when we were on our way to a church he did not have much money. I believe that he only had two dollars to get gas. And I was not getting paid from my job until the next weekend so I could not help him at the time. Well, he decided to stop at a closer gas station than where he normally would stop since he didn't have a lot of gas before we end up stranded.

When the gas station attendant came out of the station to pump the gas the first thing that the person said was,

"Hey Boy, how much gas do you need today?"

Wow! I was so mad because the person had called my Dad a boy. My Dad is a grown man that works hard and takes care of our family. So how can he get away with calling my Dad a boy?

Then the person said,

"Didn't you hear me N-----r?"

By that time, I was rising up from the car seat and was getting ready to get out of the car to tell that person to apologize to my Dad. My Dad held me firmly back with his arm and said to me under his breath,

"Just stay calm because we don't need any trouble."

"You don't know or understand what could happen to us if we try to confront him."

"So just stay calm and we can get the gas and be on our way without anyone getting hurt."

My Dad turned back towards the gas attendant and asked him to put in $2.00 worth of gas because that was all of the money that he had to spend today.

We got the gas and drove off to get to the church that my Dad was going to preach at. I was shocked to the core and fuming at what had just occurred because I did not know that people could be like that.

After that I never wanted to have to go to that gas station again! I told my Dad to never go there again because I would be afraid that something could happen to him especially if he was alone. That guy at the gas station was insulting and clearly didn't like black folks.

One night I met this very handsome guy that was about my age at this restaurant that some of my co-workers and I had eaten dinner at. His name was David Wells, and unlike me, he was white. We hit it off pretty well and started dating. He was very nice to me and took me to some of the nicest places for dinners every week over the course of several weeks.

We got along so well that I thought that maybe we could actually have a great relationship. We liked each other a lot. He was always attentive and respectful. But one night while we were driving back from a date we got stopped by a cop. The cop was not too happy at all when he saw us, because my boyfriend was a white man. It wasn't uncommon back then to pull people over based on skin color, and definitely not when two people were together that were not the same race. It isn't much different now either.

The cop searched our car with a flashlight shining so bright we couldn't see when he shoved it towards our faces. He did not say too much at first but just kept looking at us with a big ugly frown on his face. His eyes looked so mean as if he could have just shot us both dead on the spot. David and I were getting a little nervous but we knew not to say anything wrong to make the cop madder than he already was.

He looked at David and said,

"Hey… don't you think that you are in the wrong place, Sir?" Then he looked straight at me.

"Now don't you let me catch you around here in these parts again and especially not with this N----r you are with right now or you will suffer the consequences."

"Do you hear me loud and clear?"

"Now get!"

That cop scared David so bad. Apparently, this was not his first interaction with him and the same cop had spoken to him again at other times when I was not around. So, a couple of weeks later David decided that it is best that we just not see each other again for our own safety. My heart was shattered at what could have been, I cried and hated how cruel the world was. It made me so sad but after the incident happened at the gas station of how the station attendant talked to my Dad and now this cop was threatening David. Life just wasn't fair! I agreed with him that maybe we should stop dating each other; no matter how much we liked each other.

My dating life continued to not improve. One guy that I had thought was a good friend of mine named Ed had sent this strange man to my work place to meet me.

"Gloria Ann meet my friend Jack. I think that you two should get to know each other. "said Ed.

To my surprise, my friend left and this stranger stayed to talk to me. He seemed like a pretty nice guy at first. Also, wasn't bad looking. We had a great conversation. Then he told me that he would like to get to know me better while he was in town.

Apparently, he was not from town. He told me that he was just in town on business and that he would like to take me out to dinner after I get off work. I told him that a friend of my friend Ed is a friend of mine. Because I trusted Ed that he would not introduce me to anyone that would do anything bad to me I felt that I could agree to meet Jack at a restaurant to have dinner.

But after I told Jack that I could meet him for dinner, he reached down into his suit pocket and brought out what looked like a key. He tried to give me his hotel room key to come there once I was free from work! Immediately, my eyes got so big and the adrenalin in my whole entire body was about to explode with so much anger and disgust. What kind of girl did he think I was?!

I had to calm myself down quickly because I realized that I was still at work. I said to myself, "Gloria Ann just breathe, yes breathe before you speak, because you don't want to make a big scene at work and possibly get fired from your job because the noise would possibly disturb the customers."

After breathing a few times, I finally calmed down enough to tell Jack to get out and that I don't want to meet him for dinner and that I never wanted to see him ever again. I finally said,

"What kind of woman do you think I am?" I am not like that at all to go to a man's hotel room. "Are you kidding me?" "Get out of here. You are so disgusting."

Jack looked as if he saw a ghost and decided that he had better leave fast.

A few days later when my friend Ed came to see me at work I told him what Jack had done to disgust me so much and he told me that he thought that Jack was nice and had no idea that he would do what he did. So, he told me that he was very sorry and that he was not going to try to fix me up with any other men. I told Ed to promise me that he won't because even though he thinks someone would be nice, the guy may or may not have the right intentions. And in the case with this Jack person, he was just looking for a good time while he was out of town on a business trip. Ed told me that he was not going to associate with Jack anymore because he should have been more respectful to me. Especially if he wanted to have a nice date with a beautiful woman that was respectable.

A month or so after the incident with Ed's "friend," I decided to go and hang out with a couple of my girlfriends, Judy and Sheila after work on a Friday night. We went out to eat at a downtown family owned diner for cat fish and French fries, my favorite. We were talking about how there are not many good men out here to date and we did not want to have to stay single forever because we wanted to get married someday and have children, even though we were still young. We wanted what most ladies want, to raise a family and have a big house, nice car and a handsome husband. So, we decided to go driving around town like all of the other younger people did in town because it was not much else to do. Well, Judy and Sheila wanted to just sit in the car and listen to some music for a while at first, so we found a place to park.

Before long, they decided that we would have to get out of the car so the cute guys that we had just seen could see us that were parked about two cars down from where we were.

Well, there was this one guy that had his eyes on me that was handsome so I let him come over to my car to talk to me. He seemed pretty nice at first until I saw that he had this shiny something on his ring finger of his left hand. He would not let me see it and said that it was just a ring that he had gotten from his mother before she died, so he wears it. He said that it was not a big deal and that it was just a ring. But when he turned his head around the opposite way to look over to see what was happening with someone laying on their horn blaring noise, I could see that the ring was definitely a wedding ring.

When he turned back towards me, I told him that I cannot talk to him anymore because I know that he had lied to me about the ring on his finger. I told him that I don't talk to married men. He grabbed my right hand and told me that he would like to take me out to dinner and just be a friend of his and that he did not want anything else with me.

He insisted that he only wanted to be friends and to just go out to dinner with him. He even offered to pay me two hundred dollars if I were to just go out to dinner with him. I told him no and that he should be ashamed of himself of being a married man and trying to ask another woman out. Also, it was very disrespectful to me to be offering me money as if I were a prostitute.

I told him to go home to his wife and family and to just leave me alone.

I felt so bad and dirty that a man would treat me as if I were a prostitute because I was raised to respect myself, regardless of the awful thing that happened when I was little. I felt so sorry for his wife and family that he was out here trying to pick up women when he should have been home with his family. The place that my friends and I had parked our cars to hang out was where all of the young people hang out and meet new people that are our age. But I guess I had learned that everyone that is out here hanging out is not always our age anymore, nor do they have good intentions. It seems so hard to be able to trust anyone anymore.

I can reflect on another incident that happened with how men used to treat me in the past. I was beginning to date someone that I thought was a good guy named Kurt. Things were going along pretty good between us for the first few weeks but then I had gotten the opportunity to move away. Wow! He got so upset with me that I was going to be moving so far away. He was so angry that he almost punched the living room wall.

He shouted out, "We had not even had a chance to have sex yet and now you are leaving!"

After about twenty minutes of trying to calm himself down he finally told me that it is ok that I was leaving. But he wanted to ask me one thing. I told him to ask me anything because nothing can change my mind about moving away.

He asked, "Do you know another good-looking Black woman like you that he could have sex with?"

Wow! I was so shocked at what had just come out of his mouth. I was so hurt and mad at the same time because I had thought that he really liked me and wanted to truly get to know me. I liked him and wanted to get to know him better. But now I know that it was a big mistake to even have wasted all of that time going out with him for all of those weeks prior to this day.

He was a few years older than me and was a very respectable guy in town. But apparently, he is not respectable at all. At least when it comes down to woman, especially Black woman. Yes, he was a White man. By now I am beginning to wonder if that is all White men see in a Black woman is that all we are good for is to have sex with or something. I am praying that that is not going to always be the case. But I have dated some really nice White men before in my life that were nice and respectful to me.

I am getting so confused on who I can trust and who I cannot anymore. Please, God show me who I can trust and who I cannot. I am so tired of being disrespected and mistreated in this world. I just want to be loved! Can anyone ever learn to love me, be good to me and treat me nice and kind?

As the saying goes I have got to just forget about my past because every man is not going to mistreat me.

Repeat it again; every man is not going to mistreat me.

I have got to believe that there are some good men out here in this world. Yes, some that is loving, caring and kind. My Dad always told me that I need to make sure that the man that I will marry someday will be equally yoked. I don't quite understand what he means by that, but I just know that if I like a man I will go out with him and see if we are compatible and get along well. And if we can get along well and then fall in love with each other then maybe that will be the right man for me to get married to and raise a family someday.

After these events I decided that I had to move away somewhere in a big city up North and get out of the South once and for all. I had heard that there is not as much racism up in the Northern states, and thought that would solve all the world's problems in my young naïve mind. I promised myself that I would never move back to where I was born and raised again because I cannot live the way that I would want to if I stayed. There was just too much going on to stay here.

My Mom and Dad taught me that we are all human beings and one people, and constantly reminded me of God's Promise (the Spirit of Sixteen, aka John 3:16). They taught me to never be prejudice against any race and that no one should be mistreated just because of the color of their skin. God created all of us equally and loves us equally no matter what we look like.

Since I had already made up my mind to move away at some point, I got lucky and got laid off of my job. I had the opportunity to get a job in New York after I had done some searches in the paper for jobs that I could do. I finally heard back on one, and they wanted me to come (they didn't know I wasn't already there). Wow, how lucky that is, I thought.

The timing was perfect to move North! I was so done with this place! I was convinced this was the answer and would be a new start where everything just had to be better.

I packed my bags and took a flight to New York City for an interview for a job at a fancy gift boutique. It still did not pay that much money, but a little more than what I was making at the department store. The interview went well and they offered me the job. So, I took the job, told them when I could start, and went back home to pack up all of my belongings. I did not have that much stuff so I packed my car and rented a trailer to haul what didn't fit.

I stayed at a YWCA a few weeks until I found an apartment. I didn't think it through enough at the time to really plan and have everything set up before I actually moved. I was so eager to leave the South, and a place that was the source for so much pain for me at different times in my life. My new place was a very small studio apartment since the city was much more expensive than what I was used to.

After only a month of working and learning how to do my new job a few of my co-workers had invited me to go out on the town to have some fun. Their names were Tate and Loni. Both of them were so pretty—Tate with her long wavy brown hair and Loni was tall and slim with pouty lips and always changing her look with different wigs. I had not been out anywhere since arriving, so I took them up on their offer and went out dancing. I love dancing so I thought it would be fun. It felt great to let my hair down and do something I enjoyed.

The next weekend came around so we all went out dancing again but to a new place that my new friends had also not been to before. There was some kind of contest going on where if we got on stage for the competition we could win some money. Okay, I thought, I could use some extra funds especially after the move, so got closer to see what I had to do. Loni told me that all we needed to do is take off our bras and put on these white tee shirts that the club gave us. I told her "Okay," and in my naïve small-town mind couldn't think of why that was necessary. So, we put on the tee shirts and got up on the stage with all of the other women that were up there.

Well, the next thing that I knew this guy comes up on the stage and sprays cold water on us with this big garden hose. I did not like it at all. We got all wet and the water was very cold. Then Loni told me that we were supposed to walk up to the front of the stage and stick our chest out, look pretty and smile at the people down in the audience and that the judges will pick who the winners are based on who they liked the best and put on the best show.

We won $10.00 each for that degraded embarrassment! But that was disgusting and not enough money at all for what we did. I did not realize that it was actually what is called a wet t-shirt contest. Dummy me...if I would have known what it was I would not have done it! I was so young and naive coming from a small country town going into a big city and just went along with the crowd. I did not realize that I must have become friends with the kind of woman that I am not used to being around, and definitely not like how I was used to behaving. But they were the only friends that I had at the time, and I thought they were nice regardless.

Afterwards, the next club they took me to was a place to dance but then they were trying to get me to go up into these things that looked like a cage mounted above the dance floor to dance inside of it. That is when I stood up for myself and told them no that I can't and won't do that! Loni shrugged her shoulders, and she and the others got into the cages and danced, gyrating their hips to the pounding pulse of the music playing. I just stayed down on the dance floor and danced with people there.

We all were realizing that working at the small gift shop was not making us enough money to live in our apartments. So, a few weeks later Tate and Loni took me to this escort service place where one of their other friends named Sage worked. After they explained what it was, I told them that it is the same as prostitution and that I was not going to apply to get a job there.

I had heard about these places before on one of the TV shows my Momma would watch back home. They told me that it was not and that all that they would have to do is just dress up pretty and go out to dinner with these rich business men and we would make $100 per night. They said it was no big deal, and it was simple easy money.

I still told them,

"No, thanks. I don't want to do it. "I looked at the ground and stared at something invisible. This whole thing made me very uncomfortable.

"You guys, they might tell you that all you will have to do is go out to dinner or to a party with rich men but eventually, they will be asking you to be doing more and more things...more than just going out to dinner or to a party," I told them.

Tate and Loni still tried to convince me that an escort service is not the same as being a prostitute since sex wasn't involved, and all I had to do is basically go on a date with the guys and look pretty. I stuck to my guns and disagreed and Tate and Loni applied to work there. I decided to seek employment elsewhere and would figure something out.

Loni was excited when I saw her at work at the gift shop one day before she quit working with us. She told me that she went on her first escort "date" and made $100.00 plus she got a free steak dinner. She said that the man was very nice to her and that she did not have to kiss him or do anything besides just eat dinner with him and talk to him so he would not have to eat dinner alone. She thought it would be an easy job to make lots of money.

I still told her that I did not want to do that no matter how much money they would pay me because things could change eventually and it won't be just going to dinner and talking or going to parties. I told them about what I'd seen on TV before. Loni told me that I was very pretty and that I would probably make lots of money if I joined her there. She did not want me to be still struggling working at the gift boutique when I could be making almost twice as much money per day. I wished Tate and Loni good luck and I continued to search for a new job that didn't seem like such a dead end.

After a lot of persistence from me, I finally got the human resource person at one of the corporations to give me a chance at a better paying job. I got lucky and met her one day when she was trying to find a retirement gift for an employee. Ms. Tabert at first told me that since I did not have at least a two-year college degree that she cannot even give me a job application to apply at the company. I kept calling and trying to convince her to at least give me a chance to see if I could do the work.

She told me that I could only miss four problems on a math test that was given to all prospective employees to be considered for a job there. So, she had me take the math test. When she graded the test, she then handed me a job application and said,

"Congratulations! Gloria Ann, you passed the test better than some of our college educated employees. You only missed two problems out of 100. You are hired right now as soon as you can return the job application to me."

I was so excited to get this job and not have to sell my body to do it. I have great people skills and was pretty smart (or at least had always thought so). My Mom and Dad will be so proud of me. Thank you, God! I give you praise! God always takes care of me, I thought. This was a good to outweigh what could have been bad if I'd given in to the temptation of making easy money.

The Kidnapping and Assault

Chapter 6

Once I started my new job, my life was heading in the right direction, or so I thought. One day, my old friend Loni called me up crying wanting to know if we could go out dancing for old time sake because she missed my friendship. We had both been so busy, and were leading totally different lives that we had kind of lost touch. I missed her too, because we were friends and she was one of the first people that I met when I first moved to New York that was nice to me. So, I thought what would it hurt to go out dancing with an old friend and catch up on what each other is doing. Plus, I hadn't really been out in a while.

I get dressed up in my favorite burgundy colored dress with a silver chain belt that looked great against my glowing skin. I put on my large silver hoop earrings and Loni styled my hair because she was really good at doing hair. Off we went into the night life of New York City to dance until we are too tired. I was never much of a drinker, but I loved to dance, and stay out on the floor until I was exhausted. As we got out of the car Loni says to me,

"Hmm...it looks like someone already has his eyes on you girl." She nodded her head towards a guy standing up ahead by the door to the club off to her right.

"Let's slow down while we are walking to the door and just see if he will say hello to us."

I did take a quick look at him. He was fine as can be with a nice three-piece navy-blue suit, baby blue shirt, and a navy blue tie on with a nice hat. I always like a man that knows how to dress and everything is matching and on point. My oh my! And he is looking at me. Watch out now!

As Loni and I were walking past these four guys that were all dressed up and looking so fine, the one in blue that had his gorgeous eyes on me stopped me and asked me if we could talk for a little bit.

"What's your name little Angel?" he asked with a big smile on his face.

"My name is Gloria Ann." "So, what is your name?"

"My name is Terry." "Wow!" "I can hear that you must be from the South because you sure don't sound like that you are from New York," he said with a chuckle and twinkle in his eye.

"So I have found a little Angel with a Southern twang. A twang."

He laughs out loud but with a cute laugh.

"Lord, have mercy! You seem so different than most women that I have met lately." I wondered what he meant by that.

"I love different," he said.

"Do you go to college here or what do you do?" he asked.

"I work for a corporation downtown, "I answered shyly. I could barely stop smiling. I thought that he was so cute and well put together as the saying goes. I couldn't believe he was talking to me.

I asked him,

"So, what do you do, Terry?"

"Oh...well I am still in college working on my doctorate degree in medicine. Actually, I only have one more year to go. Then you can call me Dr. Terry. "

"Then I could be your doctor, right?" he added.

I just looked at him, smiled and said,

"Why not?" "It would be fine with me, Doctor Terry."

So, Terry and I talked a few minutes longer then we went inside the night club. I had forgotten all about Loni, and apparently one of the other guys was talking to her in a corner once we got inside. He bought me a drink, even though I was not old enough to drink yet. Then we danced a few times and said our good night.

"It was a pleasure meeting you my little Angel." Terry whispered softly into my ear.

"It was great meeting you, too, Doctor Terry. "I replied.

Terry yelled out, "Oh wait, let me have your phone number so I can call you tomorrow… if it is ok with you."

"Okay, it is 929-854-2328." I responded.

When I found Loni again, she was talking to a guy that she had known from her past and seemed like she was feeling a lot better than she did when we first came to the night club. I still had no idea why she was upset in the first place, but glad we got out because she seemed really down when we first arrived.

I asked Loni if she needed a ride home and she told me that she has a ride already so I can go home if I want. She gave me a big hug and said it was great seeing me. I left and headed to my car.

As I walked through the parking lot, all I could think about is how meeting Terry was a great thing because he seemed so nice and must be really smart because he is studying to become a doctor. That gave extra points on my list of finding a good man.

I believed that since he was going to become a doctor someday that he must be a nice, kind, loving and caring man that wants to help people. But I was so young and naïve. I remember my Mom always saying that I should marry a rich man so I would not have to live poor like I grew up. So, I thought that Terry would be a good catch as the saying goes. Probably not the best advice, but I didn't know any better than, as superficial as it was to think that way.

At this point, I thought that life was going to start looking even better for me. As I got into my car I was wondering if Terry would actually call me or if he would be just be like most other men and take my number and toss it in the trash and move on to the next woman that he thinks is cute. I will just go home and enjoy my day tomorrow because I have a lot of things to get done around the apartment anyway. No need to be thinking if someone that I had just met would bother to call me so soon. A lot of guys I met in the past I either never heard from, or they weren't nice anyway, except of course David…and we know how that went. Come on Gloria Ann get your head together, I thought as I was driving home.

After I got home, I recalled how some men had treated me back home.

I have got to believe that there are some good men out here in this world. Yes, someone that is loving, caring and kind, and loves God. My Dad always told me that I need to make sure that the man that I will marry someday will be equally yoked. I don't quite understand what he means by that but I just know that if I like a man I will go out with him and see if we are compatible and get along well. And if we can get along well and then fall in love with each other then maybe that will be the right man for me to get married to and raise a family someday.

So now back to meeting Terry. He seems so nice and charming. With him attending college to become a doctor, it seems promising that if he calls me and we start dating hopefully he will end up being the right man for me. My Mom would especially be so proud of me because hopefully if I could marry a doctor someday she will know that I would not have to be poor anymore and would be going up in the world instead of down.

Wow! I can't believe it; a whole month has passed by and still no phone call from Terry. Maybe he just lost my phone number or he is studying hard for his college exams or something. Oh well, that is life, I guess. The one time that I meet a man that seems like he would be good for me doesn't even call me. I started to feel very discouraged, but work definitely was keeping me busy. There was no use in getting all hung up on some guy I had only met and danced with one night anyway.

My friend Loni calls me up and asked me to go out to this new night club to help her celebrate that she is no longer with the escort service that she had worked at. I was absolutely elated at that news and happy for my friend! She decided that it was not for her at all and told me that I was right when I said that her boss would end up making her do things that she did not agree on doing.

She told me that she got a new job at a modeling agency and was making pretty good money modeling all kinds of cool clothes in the high fashion industry. I mean, this was New York City after all, so the perfect job to have here! We went out that night and guess who we saw? You guessed it. It was Terry with his charming self. Loni leans over and says to me, "Hey isn't that the guy from the last time we went out? What happened with that?" I rolled my eyes and took a sip of my drink and just shook my head.

He came over to our table where Loni and I were sitting and gave me the excuse that he did not call me because he was busy with school and studying around the clock, and that he had also lost my phone number. He told me that he was very sorry.

He promised to take me out soon and wanted me to give him my number again. I wrote down my phone number for him slowly. But this time I watched him actually put the paper that I wrote my number on inside of his wallet. So hopefully he will not lose it this time around!

He asked me to dance, and as soon as we were getting ready to get up to dance there were two women fighting in the club, and everyone was crowded in a circle around them, when one of them pulled out a gun. I was so frightened that I just froze and did not know what to do. There were a few people screaming. I started praying to God silently that he will protect us and that no one will get hurt. Terry told us to just stay calm and don't move because you never know what can happen in situations like this. They both struggled with the gun. Then suddenly, the gun got loose and slid across the table right in front of us. By then we all got up from the table and ran for cover. But fortunately, the women stopped fighting and the manager took the gun and had security to escort the women out of the club. Then things went back to normal as if nothing had happened. I was so glad it didn't turn out worse.

The DJ started playing a nice slow song so Terry asked me to come and dance with him on that one.

It was nice dancing with him so close. He told me that I was a very good dancer. I told him thank you and smiled while looking up into his gorgeous dark brown eyes. His eyes were like hypnotizing me or something. I could not explain it. We danced to a few more songs that night, and I was feeling great on my way home.

The next day was Sunday morning and my telephone rang. It was Terry.

"Hello my sweet angel", he said in a very soft voice. "Did you have a good night's sleep?

"Yes, I did," I replied.

"Would you like to go out to eat breakfast with me?"

"Sure," I answered.

"Ok, so come and pick me up at my friend John's house on Elliot Street in about an hour. Hold on and I will give you the address. Sorry, but I forgot to tell you that I don't have a car because on campus we aren't allowed to have cars so I don't have one here. But I do know how to drive and I have my driver's license. So, no worries." He gave me John's address, and I told him I would be there within an hour.

I jumped into the shower and got dressed so fast. I know that I should not be acting like this but I am so excited to be going out to breakfast with Terry today! I am so attracted to him that I can't wait to get to know him and see if he is the right man for me. The usually over cautious me was definitely forgotten for the time being!

When I drove up to the house, Terry was already waiting for me outside. He was smiling so big and seemed very happy to see me. He told me that I looked beautiful, which made me blush.

We went to this little diner near where he lived. He told me that he loves to go to the restaurants that are near where he lives since he does not have a car right now, and they all had great food. So, he walks to where he needs to go or some of his friends will drive him around or he will take the bus, which is what most people do in NYC anyway.

The breakfast was amazing and I ordered another favorite, steak grilled medium well, scrabble eggs, hash brown potatoes and coffee with cream and sugar. It was delicious. Terry asked me all kinds of questions about where I grew up, especially because I had this strong country accent. He told me that I was the sweetest woman that he has ever met before. He told me that he liked me a lot already, and loved my big appetite. He was so upbeat, and seemed so different than how many of my dates previously have been.

After breakfast was over he asked me if I would like to go dancing this weekend. And I told him that I would love to. He also asked me if I could come and pick him up again because his friend, John was going to be going out of town. I told him that I would.

I dropped Terry off at his place and went back home.

I excitedly called Loni up and told her about my breakfast with Terry and what a great time we had laughing and learning a little about one another. I also told her we plan to go out dancing at the club this weekend coming up. Loni was so happy for me that hopefully Terry and I will hit it off well and will have a good relationship together at some point in the future because she knows that I have not had many good relationships in the past.

I was so excited! The week passed by so fast and it was time to get ready for my big date with Terry. I put on my prettiest dress that was the colors of the sky and the sun. It also had this gold chain belt that looked perfect with it. I put on my gold star shaped earrings and left my flowy hair down. My hair was wavy and as black as coal now because I had just colored it black even though my natural hair color is kind a shade of brown. I wanted to look beautiful for Terry.

It was going on 7:30 pm so I had to hurry up and get out the door to pick him up. I drove to Elliot Street and again Terry was already waiting for me outside. Hmm…I thought to myself that it was a little odd that he always waits outside for me and never lets me come to the door and ring the doorbell? Oh, well, maybe he is just so excited to see me as I am of him so he just sees my car and comes outside.

Terry was decked out in a very nice dark grey suit with a matching dark grey dress hat and super shiny black dress shoes. As I've already said, I love a man that wears nice suits and nice shoes. I can do without him wearing the hat, though. I think a good-looking man wearing a nice suit and nice shoes is so sexy, and Terry was definitely that today!

"Hi my sweet Angel," Terry said with his sparkling smile. "Let's get out of here. By the way, you look so beautiful tonight. You must have gotten all dressed up for me."

He looked at me and gave me a quick wink. As I started up the car, he gave me a soft gentle kiss. His lips were so soft. I loved it when he kissed me because it felt so much different than what I had experienced in the past, even though this was only our second time going out. Thanks to God for sending me this very nice handsome man, I thought.

We arrived at the nightclub and it was very crowded this time—even more than the last time we were there. I wonder what is going on that it was so over crowded. Oh, of course, there is a live band playing the music tonight, and it was more upbeat. This was definitely my thing, and I was ready to dance all night! This is so exciting to me because I had not been to a nightclub that had a live band playing great music like this in a while.

I love all kinds of music and this band was awesome. Rock to the beat of the music, yes, rock to the beat of the music. The band had everyone in the place dancing like it was nobody's business. It was so much fun, and we were smiling, sweating and dancing all night.

Terry told me that if I like music so much that he can play some of his music collection if I want sometime. He asked if he could come over to my place sometime soon and he will play me some of his kinds of music. I told him that I would love to.

We danced until about 1:00 am that night. Then I told him that I must be getting back because I wanted to attend church the next morning. He seemed surprised that I wanted to go, but said that it was okay if I wanted to take him back home. So, we left the nightclub and I drove Terry back to his place. He got out of the car and just walked to his door and went inside.

Wow! I thought, what is going on with him that he forgot to kiss me goodnight? Oh well, he had given me a nice kiss when we started this date so I am not going to complain. Maybe he was just preoccupied for some reason. Anyway, I had a great time because I was with him and I love to dance.

A couple of weeks went by and I had not heard anything from Terry. I wondered what was going on with him to not call me at all for two whole weeks. You know the saying…If a man does not call you in a while then that must mean that he has lost interest in you and has found another woman. Darn! I sure hope that this is not the case that he has lost interest in me now, especially after we had a few dates where we really enjoyed each other's company and it seemed like we had a lot in common. I didn't understand how someone could be so eager, and then completely ghost me.

I thought that he truly liked me a lot, but I guess that I was wrong. He had mentioned to me that he wanted to play some of his kinds of music at my place sometime. I wonder if my friend Loni has seen him out anywhere lately. She goes out way more than I do, especially since she has a much more glamorous job than I do. I will give her a call right now.

My phone rings…it is Terry.

"Hello my sweet Angel," Terry said in a very low scratchy voice.

I didn't respond. I was furious and glad at the same time. He definitely owed me an explanation for just disappearing.

"Sorry, but I have been a little busy in the past couple of weeks so I could not call you."

Silence.

"You know that I have studying to do for finals amongst other things."

I'm still not responding.

"Please forgive me. I will make it up to you, I promise."

I was not too happy about him waiting so long to call me after we had so much fun in the prior weeks after he seemed like he was getting to like me a lot more. I think he should have at least given me a quick call the first week to let me know that he would be busy studying rather than just going radio silent. Men could be so inconsiderate!

I paused for a few seconds before I responded to him.

"Oh, hello Terry," I answered. "Good to finally hear from you."

"No worries, I forgive you...this time."

Terry's voice started to clear up a little better as we talked. He finally asked me when would be a good time for me to come to pick him up and he can have a music date and I listen to some of his collection. I told him that tomorrow night would be a good night for me since it will be Friday. It had been a long week, and I didn't really feel like going out on the town anyway.

Well, Friday night rolls around, but Terry had not called yet to let me know what time I should be picking him up at his place. It is already 8:00 p.m. Here we go again, I thought. This guy is no different than the rest of the flaky ones. He finally calls me at about 8:45 p.m. and he tells me that he has run into a big problem and wanted to know if I could let him stay at my place until he can find a new place to live! He sounded so sad and upset. He told me that unfortunately, his roommate had kicked him out. He said that they had gotten into a big fight and that he had to get out of there by midnight tonight.

I got very quiet for a minute and did not know what to say or do at that moment. All of this was sitting really weird with me. I remember my parents taught me to never live with a man when you are not married to him because it is not right in the eyes of God.

I just thought that maybe I could let him sleep on the couch for a few days. Yes, it is just for a few days I am sure. So, I told Terry that yes, if he did not mind sleeping on my couch because I was not ready for him to sleep in my bed. After all, we had not really known each other for very long. None of this was sitting right with me, but my parents also taught me to help those in need, so my very naïve self agreed to help him out.

I told Terry that I could come and pick him up at about 10:00 p.m. because I had a couple of things to do first. He told me that it would be fine with him.

So, I got a sheet and blanket from the closet and took one of my pillows off of my bed and put everything together on the couch. I wanted to make sure things were in place before I bring him to my place so when he sees that I already have the couch ready for him that maybe I would not have to worry about him trying to come into my bed. Even though I liked him a lot I still was not ready to go sleeping with him in my bed yet, and after my experiences, I wasn't exactly the most trustful of men in the first place since most only seemed interested in one thing.

While driving to pick up Terry, I still felt like maybe something else is wrong that he was not telling me. You know when they say if your intuition tells you that something is wrong then you need to listen to it. I felt so uneasy, but went completely against my instincts.

I finally pull up to Elliot Street and the lights were kind of dim looking or maybe it was not bright in Terry's place because some of the lights could be turned off or something.

I walk slowly up to the door and ring the doorbell.

Terry comes to answer the door and lets me inside. When I got inside and was looking around there were things thrown all over the place. It was a mess. I wonder what all had happened there. He says to hold on a couple of minutes so he can finish packing up some of his things.

As he was packing I was a little puzzled because as I walked around more I kept seeing these little drops of blood everywhere. That definitely made doubt start to creep in a bit. Curiosity got the best of me, so I had to ask him (especially since I was about to let this man in my home),

"Hey, Terry, Why is there drops of blood everywhere?"

Terry answered,

"Oh, I got a little hot because it was hot in here earlier and I had a bad nose bleed. You know how sometimes your nose might bleed if you get too hot. But I am fine now; I just need to clean up the mess." I eyed him warily.

"No worries, everything is fine. Nothing to worry about. It was just a little nose bleed and that's all, baby."

"What about your roommate?" I asked.

"We did not have a fist fight or anything like that so don't worry about it. He isn't here so I could have a chance to get out. We just had a disagreement and decided we didn't need to live in the same place anymore. No biggie, except it happened so fast."

"I just got to get out of here. "

"Thank you so much for coming to pick me up and let me stay with you for a while until I can find a new place to live."

"It is so sweet of you, my Angel."

It did not take very long for Terry to finish packing up his things. He only had a couple of suitcases, four boxes of books and one box of music albums.

He gave me a hug and said,

"Now let's get out of here. I don't care if I ever see this place again."

I helped Terry carry out his things to my car so it could go faster and we could leave. He seemed a little agitated as we were packing up the car. But once that was all done he became calmer.

"Thank you so much, my sweet Angel," Terry whispered into my right ear.

Then he said,

"Man! If it were not for you coming to rescue me there is no telling what would have happened."

"I am so thankful for you, my sweet Angel. "

As we were driving back to my place Terry hardly said anything else to me. But I just let things be nice and quiet so he would not have the chance to get agitated again. I could tell he was stressed out and still angry. That was a side of him that I had not seen before. But I figured that he would tell me about what all happened tonight, or whenever he decides to tell me.

I was even thinking about that I never got to meet his old roommate. I had assumed that it was a he because, why on earth would he be going out on dates with me if he was living with a woman? That would not be a good idea at all so I just did not want to even think about it in that way. At least he doesn't have to worry about his old roommate because now he has me. I told myself I was silly for thinking that, and it was just my imagination running wild because of my own past insecurities.

Even though I did not feel too comfortable about having a man stay at my place at first, I finally got used to it after about a week. He was much calmer the next morning after that first night when I picked him up. Terry was good about sleeping on the couch so I thought that I did not have anything to worry about. He was so nice and charming to me and did not try to get out of the ordinary at all. He was helpful and did his part to keep everything orderly in my tiny apartment, so I really appreciated that!

But then one day we had to go out and get more groceries. As we got out of the car and started walking on the sidewalk to the store a couple of people that passed us said hello. Then I said hello back to them and they smiled at us. I smiled back but Terry did not. Shortly before we got to the grocery store door an older man that was probably in his seventies wearing an old beat up grey hat and raggedy clothes said hello to us and smiled. I said hello and smiled back at him just to be nice like I did the previous people that passed by us. But Terry became so agitated that he just burst out this really loud scream at me.

"Are you serious, woman?! He shouted at me with furious eyes.

I asked him, "What are you talking about?"

"What are you doing flirting with another man when I am standing right here with you? Don't you ever disrespect me like that again? Do you hear me woman?" He was squeezing my arm really hard and it was starting to hurt.

I was so shocked and frightened that I just froze for a few seconds. Then I said to him in a soft voice because I did not want to cause a scene,

"I was not flirting at all. I was just saying hello back to a man that said hello to us. That is just being a polite person."

"Hey, I am only 20 years old so why would I be flirting with an old man that is old enough to be my grandfather anyway? Just think about what you are saying, Terry." I put my shaking hand on his to try to get him to loosen his grip on me.

"Please calm down. I don't like this side of you at all. What is wrong with you?" I asked.

Terry just flipped out on me and became this person that I did not even know at all. I prayed to God that he would calm down and things would be back to normal. But he yelled out at me again,

"Hey woman, you are not as beautiful as you think that you are, either. "

"You are not the best-looking woman in this world because I know other women that look a lot better than you."

After a couple of minutes, he seemed to snap out of it and finally calmed down and apologized to me, flashing his usual dazzling smile. He told me that he really did not mean it. He said that he was getting jealous because I am his woman and he doesn't want to ever share me with another man. He told me that he just lost it for a minute and that he is not always like this.

Terry was so nice to me and back to his regular self after we finally got inside of the grocery store. We shopped for our favorite foods, played around racing the cart around the store like two kids, and drove back home laughing and joking like nothing bad had happened. I just figured that maybe he was just having a bad day or something because ever since he moved out of his old place he has been a little off.

I don't like that agitated side of him and it scares me. I don't like any yelling or screaming at all. I began to pray that this behavior is just a temporary thing. Please, God don't let this side of Terry come out ever again. Just let it be that he is having a bad day for some reason or another.

I cooked a great meal of chicken and rice with spinach and lemon cake for dessert. Terry loved it. He finally unpacked a couple of his music albums that he wanted me to hear so we listened to music for a little while. He was so nice and kind to me for the rest of the night. And yes, he was still sleeping on my couch.

The next morning Terry even asked me if I would like to go to this new church that a friend of his had told him about. I told him that it would be a nice thing for us to do, especially since I had not gone to church in a while since he came into my life. By the way, he never tells me any of his friend's names anymore for some reason.

We drove to the church with the radio on to hear some old-time gospel music. I figured the music can help clear the air and we would have a pleasant drive as it was a little far to drive. I wanted to ask him who his friend was that told him about this church but I was afraid to. I did not want to get him agitated. But after that day at the store, he started to really change into this other person that I don't know at all. He was starting to seem like he would get irritated at the tiniest things. I just didn't get it. At the same time, I don't like having to walk on egg shells. If I want to ask my boyfriend a question I should be able to ask him, right?

Oh well, maybe I won't ask him because it is not really important to know I guess. We should just enjoy the service. And later I am going to cook a nice meal and it will make him happy because he loves my cooking. A little while back he had told me that my food is better than everyone else's

I think I will bake a peach cobbler for dessert because I had not made that for Terry yet. I just know that he will love it. I will have to check to see if we have all of the ingredients first before I tell him that we are going to have it for dessert today.

We arrive at the church on time because it is 11:00 a.m. on the dot. Terry opens the car door and helps me get out. I told him thank you and he gave me a big smile and winked at me. He is acting like his old sweet and kind self right now. I like this side of him and I pray that he stays this way.

The church service was awesome. I like this church and hope that we can come back again sometime soon.

Terry told me that he liked the church service, too. We held hands as we walked back to the car, smiling the whole way. When God is in the house everything is fine. We both enjoyed a great day. I cooked dinner and yes, we did have all of the ingredients to make a peach cobbler. Everything went so well and I was happy that the day was going great. He said that he was as full as a stuffed turkey. He started laughing so hard at the thought. It was so much fun to see him in such a great mood for a change. At about 9:30 p.m. Terry kissed me good night and went to sleep on the couch and seemed fine. I was so glad of that. It is so good to be able to have a peaceful night.

On Monday I was off work but Terry had to go to college so he just took the bus there and was ok with doing that. But I would usually drop him off at the campus on my way to work when I am working.

But after that day, he started to really change into this other person that I don't know at all. He was starting to seem like he would get irritated at the tiniest things. I just didn't get it.

When Terry got home from college he seemed very tired and told me that he was going to take a nap. I told him that it was okay with me if he would like to take a nap in my bed. Of course, you know that he took me up on that deal. He had wanted to sleep in my bed for a good while now. For the past couple of months, I had him to sleep on the couch but today I decided that maybe I was ready to let him sleep in my bed. God forgive me but I am ready for him to make love to me. He was so nice lately that I thought maybe this is the time. And then we would know if we are compatible to really be a committed couple.

As Terry went into the bedroom I followed right behind him. He had taken his shoes, socks and the rest of his clothes off then went into the bathroom to take a shower and I followed him in there, too. He began to undress me by unzipping my dress and it fell to the floor quickly. As he was unhooking my bra he kissed me gently and ever so softly on my neck and shoulders. Then kissed me on down my back then he turned me around and kissed me gently on the lips. I was getting so hot and wet that I could hardly stand it.

I kissed Terry so softly and we ended up making love in the shower. Then again by the time we got back into the bedroom. It was a very blissful night for sure.

I had hoped that we would have more nights like that one. I loved it when he was in a good mood like he was that night. But things started changing with his behavior again soon thereafter. We had a few wonderful blissful nights but it did not last very long.

He begins going out by himself to the nightclub while I was still at work on some early evenings. I did not like to have to work late after the regular hours but sometimes I had no choice. I did not question him about going out alone without me because maybe he just needed to wind down from college because I know that he had to study a lot.

I called my friend Loni and told her that it was beginning to get to me a little knowing that Terry is going out without me with him.

She told me to just not worry about it because it is normal for a man to want to go out with his friends sometime just to unwind. She told me not to make such a big deal out of it. So, I tried hard not to let it get to me.

I don't know maybe because I don't trust too many people, but it is making it hard for me to trust him. Because for him to go out as many times as he has lately I am wondering if I can truly trust him to not be cheating on me. I would hate it if he is out there cheating on me with another woman. I have done so much for him, especially letting him come and stay with me when he had no place else to go. But I am afraid to start questioning him on why he is going to the nightclub so much and not waiting until I get home so we can go out together. I don't know what to think or what to do right now. God help me. Show me what I should do. I need you God. Please help me! I know that someone has to be taking him there unless he is taking the bus to get there.

Several more nights pass that Terry goes out to the nightclub without me. He is also not being romantic with me anymore as much as he was. So, I believe that he is either cheating on me or maybe he just does not want me in his life anymore. But he should just pack up and leave if that is what he really wants. He should not be disrespecting me and my kindness to him.

I just don't know what to do if he continues to go out like this without me. Maybe I will see if my boss at work can change my work schedule around so I don't end up having to work as many days late. Yes, maybe that will work. I will check with my work tomorrow because I cannot keep feeling like this.

After a few weeks Terry is staying more at home than going out without me since I was able to get my work schedule changed a little to not have to work too many days late.

And Terry and I are doing better. Now when we want to go out to the nightclub we will both go out together. I think that it is so much better that we go out together than for either of us to go out alone. Because if either of us goes out alone too many times then I know that it will just lead to more troubles in our relationship. Clearly, we both had some insecurity.

A month later I am in the kitchen cooking some pancakes for dinner on a Friday night because it was something quick and easy to do after working a late day at work. Yes, I was just too tired to cook anything else. Suddenly, the phone rings and since I was in the middle of cooking dinner I had asked Terry if he could answer the phone because I was busy.

The phone keeps ringing a few more times then Terry picks up the phone.

Terry answers, "Hello."

"Hello, is Gloria Ann there?" A man speaks from the other end of the phone.

"Who is this?" Terry replies.

"Did you hear me? Who is this?" Terry screams into the phone.

"My name is David and I would like to speak with Gloria Ann if she is there. I am an old friend of hers. "

"And who are you, may I ask?" Asked David.

"I am her boyfriend you knucklehead! Don't you ever call her again or you will be sorry!" Shouted Terry.

Terry hung up the phone in a huge rage. He was so angry. I thought that he was going to break my phone because he was so mad.

"Who was that on the phone, Terry?" I asked in a shaky voice.

Terry replied, "It was some man asking for you." "What are you doing, Gloria Ann?" "You have been cheating on me for all of this time, haven't you?"

"No, I have not." I replied.

"Oh yes you have because, why would some guy be calling you just out of the blue after all of this time?" He shouted. His fists were clenched and I could see his veins bulging in his forehead.

"I have been with you for about four months now and all of a sudden after you have stopped working late a guy just up and calls you like this?" Terry screamed louder.

"I swear on a whole stack of Bibles that I have not been cheating on you."

"I am telling you the truth that I am not cheating on you," I choked out in a shaky voice.

"Please believe me," I said while crying elephant tears.

"I have no reason to be cheating on you. I am a one-man woman and don't cheat on anyone that I am with."

"I don't believe in seeing anyone else when I am with someone."

"Please believe me, please. I am telling you the truth."

"Ok, then prove it." Terry screamed out even louder.

"I am going to make you a joint mixed with something special for you in it and you are going to smoke it in front of me."

"This Angel Dust will be just the thing for you. If you are telling me the truth then you will smoke it for me."

"You know that I don't smoke anything!" I cried out. "Please don't make me do that. Please don't."

Terry made the joint and put it up to my mouth and grabbed me by the neck with one hand and tried to force me to smoke it with his other hand. It got into my mouth but I could not smoke it. I kept spitting it out and he would just pick it back up and try again. Then he punched me in my stomach super hard several times.

I screamed as loud as I could. I was in horrible pain like way back when I was a little girl.

"God help me! God help me, please help me. Somebody please help me!"

Then he grabbed me by the neck and started choking me. He choked me so hard that I almost passed out. I felt like he was squeezing every breath out of me as I struggled to breathe. He then slammed me real hard up against the wall and caused my head to bang violently against it, my beautiful black hair flailing wildly. He ripped my shirt off and beat my face several times until blood came gushing out of my mouth. The blood was running down my face onto my neck and chest. I just wanted him to stop. I couldn't believe what was happening and I hurt so badly. Why was God letting this happen?

I could feel my eyes swelling up. The glasses I had on had broken and fell onto the floor.

I thought that if he punches me any harder that I was going to die for sure. There was blood everywhere. I was afraid that he was going to kill me right then and there. He was in such an angry rage and out of his mind. My head began to pound with pain so bad that I felt like a freight train hit me.

I cried so hard until I could not cry anymore and my legs gave out so I fell down onto the floor. By that time, I believed that I must have passed out. Because I did not wake up until about 1:00 a.m. in the morning. I clawed and drug my mangled body down to the bathroom. I could hardly pull myself up to the sink. And when I looked into the mirror with my limited vision since I didn't have my glasses and one eye had completely swollen shut, I could not believe what I saw. I told myself that it was not me. This cannot be me. My face is ruined. God help me. I did not recognize the face staring back at me in that mirror.

My right eye was completely shut and my left eye I could see a little out of it. My lips were swollen and cut. They had hard dried up blood on them from where they must have been bleeding.

My stomach felt so sore and I was so nauseated that I had to throw up in the toilet. My throat was so sore from being choked. I felt like just dying so I would not have to feel all of the pain that I was in. Terry was still there and came into the bathroom to apologize to me of what he had done. He told me that he was so sorry and to please forgive him, but that he just got so jealous when David called for me and he just lost it. He didn't know what had come over him. He promised me that he would never hurt me like this again.

Terry had me lay down on the bed to try to get some sleep. He told me to just go to sleep and that I will feel all better in the morning. I laid my head down on the pillow but I just could not go to sleep. I kept having nightmares of him beating me. I did not want him anywhere near me. He is a monster!

No, this cannot be happening to me. Not me! I started asking myself, how can a man be so nice and kind to me then just turn on me like a dime like he did? I must have been so naïve! At least this is the weekend so I will have a couple of days to try to put ice packs on my face and body to take some of the swelling down hopefully before I have to go back to work. I am still in so much pain though so I hope I will be able to work without anyone noticing how beat up my face is. Maybe I can wear some sun glasses and tell my co-workers that I have been having problems with my eye because of sun burn or an allergy or something.

I must make myself get some sleep. At about 3:00 a.m. in the morning I finally fell asleep. When I woke up at about 12:00 p.m. noon my head was throbbing with so much pain that I could hardly lift my head up. So, I just laid there on the bed a few more minutes to try to get myself to get the strength to get out of bed.

I finally got myself up and Terry was still asleep on the couch so I went to try to sneak out of the door to leave but there was the heavy dresser that he must have pushed up against the door so I would not leave. It was way too heavy for me to try to move it over to be able to open the door so I just went back into the bedroom and laid back down. Please help me God. What am I going to do? I have to leave. I cannot stay here because I am afraid that Terry might get into another angry rage and beat me up again. I don't think that I could survive to be beaten up again. No, I cannot take it. I'm a prisoner in my own home. I was so angry and in so much pain.

I must find a way to get out of here as fast as I can, I kept thinking. But that dresser is too heavy for me to move it out of the way.

I just have to see what else I can do to get out of here. I can't go out of any of the windows because it is seven stories down to the street. So that is certainly not an option. I hear a noise that sounds like it is coming from the kitchen. It sounded like pots and pans being tossed around and some falling down onto the floor. Oh wait…now I can hear something that sounds like glass breaking. I stayed very quiet in the bedroom still lying on the bed. The noise was getting so loud that I had to cover my ears. What on earth is he doing in there? I wonder what he is going to do next.

Terry finally comes stomping into the bedroom and asks me,

"Where is your egg turner thing?" You know that thing that you turn over an egg when you make a fried egg?

"It should be in the second drawer from the left side of the cabinets next to the stove." I answered.

Terry goes back into the kitchen to look for the egg turner. I hear more noises. This time it sounds like he is throwing out the cooking utensils out of the drawer onto the counter top.

"Well, I have not found it yet." He yells out. "And it is not in there where you said that it was. "

"Get yourself up out of that bed right now, you lazy ugly good for nothing piece of trash!" He shouted out super loud.

"I am trying to cook some eggs so I can eat because I am hungry right now."

"I was going to try to do it myself since you were still sleeping. At least you were in there awfully quiet like you were asleep. "

"I really feel so bad that I beat you up last night. I truly did not mean to."

"I don't know what came over me."

"I got so jealous of that guy calling you just out of the blue like that."

"Please forgive me, my little Angel."

"I promise you with sugar on top that I will never lay a hand on you like that again."

"Say that you forgive me."

"Say it."

"I can't hear you."

"Say it."

He literally had just gone from a full-on rage to the sweet-sounding Terry that I thought I knew. After a couple of minutes had passed I finally told Terry that I forgive him. I felt like if I don't say that I forgive him that he would get angrier at me and just start his barrage on me like last night all over again. I would rather just agree with what he wants me to say or do to keep the peace. I felt so trapped.

I finally get up out of the bed and I slowly walk into the kitchen and find the egg turner on the top of the counter top. Apparently, Terry was so upset that when he was throwing out the utensils he had also thrown out the egg turner and did not notice it.

"Since you got me out of the bed I will go ahead and cook something to eat because I am hungry, also. We both need to eat something, "I said.

He put his arms around me and kissed me gently on my forehead. He told me that everything was going to be alright and that he was so sorry. Terry had turned into this person I couldn't put a name on. I guess you would call it a Jekyll/Hyde personality. One minute he was this nice, charismatic, gentle man but then he can turn into this mean maniac monster at the drop of a dime.

I don't like the mean monster guy at all and don't know what to do to get him out of my apartment now. I feel that I am stuck now. He has that heavy dresser blocking me from leaving. I don't know what he is trying to do to me. Is he trying to make me be his punching bag to release all of his anger out on me or what? God, I pray to you to help me. Please help me.

I picked up the pots and pans from the floor and put them into the kitchen sink so I can wash them after we eat. Then I gathered up the utensils and put everything back into their proper places inside of the cabinet drawer. I remembered hearing glass break so I looked around to see what was broken.

It looks like he threw a water glass down onto the floor and it broke. So, I took the broom and dust pan out of the tiny closet near the kitchen and swept up the glass and tossed it into a paper grocery bag then into the trash can.

Terry had finally calmed down and we had a good breakfast of fried eggs and toast with orange juice. I did not bother to brew any coffee because that would have taken a little longer and I wanted to get breakfast over with as soon as I could. It hurt so bad to try and open my mouth to eat and I struggled to try to put food in. I wondered if my jaw was broken.

"Well, what are we going to be doing today, Terry?" I asked.

"I have not decided yet." He answered.

"Maybe we could just stay in and watch some movies."

"You look pretty beat up, especially in your face."

"I don't want anyone to see you and get any crazy ideas."

"You know how when people look at things they start to thinking the wrong kinds of things when they have no idea what really went on with us," he said, as if something else actually occurred other than the obvious.

"No one needs to even know that I put my hands on you. It's your fault anyway for making me mad."

"And you better not ever tell anyone because I know where to find you."

"I will never hurt you like that again. Remember that I had promised you and I really mean it. "

"You can trust me."

"I won't ever punch you again."

"That person was not me because I don't do things like beating up on a woman."

"Remember I am going to college to save lives and not take lives."

Terry began to sound like he really means it that he will not hurt me again. Hmm…but will I really be able to trust him now? I just don't know what to do. I want to get out of here and go somewhere that I know that I will be safe. But, he swears it will never happen again. Part of me wants to believe him, but my instincts tell me otherwise. But with that dresser in the way I will have to try to convince him somehow to go shopping or something to get out of the apartment so I can think.

Terry was certainly not going to be trekking out anywhere today because he knows if anyone sees me the way that I look right now that they would find out that he beat me up really bad. My eyes are starting to look slightly better and not as swollen but it will take a few days before I can possibly wear a pair of very dark sunglasses so no one will see my eyes.

I asked Terry,

"Why did you put that heavy dresser in the way blocking the door that we cannot open the door to get out of here?"

He answered, "Because I wanted to. That way I can keep you in here so you can't go running off and telling anyone what happened."

"I know how you are with your mouth. You would go running to Loni and whomever else out here that you know."

"Eventually, everyone in the whole city would know about it and it would ruin my reputation and my whole life. "

"I just can't take that risk of you getting out of here and running your mouth. "

"There is no way that I am going to let you ruin my life little lady."

"So just get that thought out of your head right now."

He continued,

"No, I am not going to let you leave out that door."

"At least not yet. I need to make sure that you are not going to be talking to anyone about this."

"You better get this ingrained into your mind right now…Don't you dare tell anyone what happened here inside of your apartment or you will be very sorry! And you mark my word I mean it!"

I became so scared that he is going to hurt me again. So, I went into the living room and sat down quietly on the couch and did not say a word. I really did not know what to do at that point but to just sit and be quiet.

I told him that I promise that I would not tell anyone as long as I lived in that place because I don't want to ruin his life. I told him that I loved him so he could calm down. After he had calmed down he told me that he wanted to marry me. He told me that he really did not mean to hurt me and that he just got out of control of his anger. He made a promise to me that he would work on trying to control his anger problems.

Terry came over to the couch and sits down beside me and promised that if I marry him that everything would be just fine. Apparently, he thought that if we got married that he would own me and that he would not have to be in an angry jealous rage ever again because I would belong to him and to him only.

Well, I don't want to be owned by anyone let alone a man, who hurt me, brutally beat me and is not allowing me to leave my own apartment. That means that he is keeping me here against my will, which is the same as false imprisonment. He surely must not be thinking straight right now.

How could he not know that he is holding me against my will? False imprisonment is what it is called, but to me and the way that I feel I call it kidnapping me? What on earth is he thinking? He must think that I am stupid or something if he thinks that I am not going to get out of this place and leave sooner or later.

I may be from a little small country town up in the mountains but I do have common sense. I must think of some way to keep him calm enough for me to be able to get out of here.

Otherwise, there is no telling what he will do to me that he has not already done. I actually feel lucky that I am still alive right now. Because he was in such a jealous rage that I believe that he could have killed me that night that he beat me up. Terry was totally out of his mind or something. I never thought that he would have done such a thing to me.

I have certainly learned that you can't judge a book by its cover. I was so thankful that God saved me from any other harm. To God be the glory! Thank you, God, for saving me. I always live by what I call The Spirit of Sixteen. It is the Holy Bible verse taken from the King James Version in the book of John chapter 3 verse 16;

For God so loved the world that he gave his only begotten son that whosoever believeth in him should not parish but have everlasting life.

I pray that God continues to save me from any more harm. I am still in some pain from my injuries. It has now been two days after I have missed work. I must be able to at least call in to my work and tell them something as to why I have not been at work or I could lose my job. I have a great job and I just cannot afford to lose it. So, I must try to convince Terry to let me call out to my work and tell them that I have been sick or something.

I knelt down on my prayer stand that I had brought from my hometown in the mountains when I first moved into my apartment. I feel that I need lots of prayers to help me get through this trauma. Certainly nothing on Earth was going to get me through this.

"Dear Lord, please hear me today as I pray. I pray for your strength and guidance to help me stay safe and get out of this terrible relationship and situation that I have gotten myself into. I pray in the name of the Father, the Son and the Holy Spirit, Amen!"

Thank you, Lord, for all that you have done for me. I love my prayer stand. It helps me to calm down right now as I am wondering what I can do to get out of this situation. I went back into the bedroom and laid down on the bed and cried quietly myself to sleep.

I woke up the next morning still feeling lots of pain. But at least the swelling of my eyes has gone down a lot to almost normal looking again. My mouth was still sore from the cuts on my lips. And my chest feels like I need to go and possibly get some x-rays in case I have some broken ribs. I don't feel well at all.

Yikes! This is the fourth day that I have now missed going into work. I am hoping I am not fired after all the work I'd done at this job and hours I had put in to get promoted and everything! I must call my boss and let him know that I have been sick and not able to work this week. I have to call in today for sure; otherwise, I was sure I would lose my job.

I got up out of bed and tip-toed into the living room very quietly because I did not want to make Terry any angrier than he is already. I spoke to him as calmly and as sweetly as I could.

"Terry, please let me call in to my boss at work to let him know that I have been too sick this week to come to work. If I don't call in today I can lose my job. I won't be able to pay the rent and the rest of the bills if I don't have a job."

Terry looked at me and thought for a few minutes then he finally handed me the phone and told me that I can only make this one call and then I must hang up quickly.

He had this evil look in his eyes as he handed me the phone and said,

"Hey, for all I know I bet your boss had been looking at your beautiful legs or something and that is the only reason why he had given you a good raise this year. I don't trust him the way that I saw him looking at you at the company party that you had taken me to a few weeks ago."

"Yes, I never did mention it to you back then because I was more under control of my anger at the time but now I don't trust anyone around you because you belong to me and no one else can or will ever have you if I have anything to do with it."

"Trust me, I mean no one else can have you, but me."

I tried to keep as calm as I could while I was dialing my work phone number. I actually wanted to scream into the phone, "Help me…I am being held against my will."

But I just kept calm and asked to speak to my boss, Mr. Bayport.

"Hello, with whom am I speaking with?" He asked.

"Oh, hello, Mr. Bayport, this is Gloria Ann Freely. I am so sorry but I have been so sick this week and had not been well enough to talk on the phone until today."

"Please forgive me for not calling you sooner to let you know that I have been too sick to come into work. But I hope that I will be well enough to come in next Monday. "

Mr. Bayport replied. "Well, I am glad that you are doing better and did call me today."

"We were all worried about what could be going on with you because it is not like you to not come into work."

"You are one of our best employees so I thought that it must be something wrong for you not to show up to work for a whole week."

"We hope you get well soon and we will see you on Monday."

"Take care."

I was so happy that Mr. Bayport seemed to understand that I was too sick to make it into work this past week. So, I felt a little better that now I won't lose my job. As long as I could show up on Monday morning, everything would be fine.

As soon as I hung up the phone, Terry's eyes were so angry looking that I thought that he was going to hit me with the phone but he looked sideways then gave the phone and phone cord a good pull. He used all of his strength and yanked the phone right out of the wall. Pieces of sheet rock scattered around everywhere so I had to move out of the way quickly to dodge from getting hit with some of it.

I became very frightened because I did not know what he was going to do to me now. The phone is broken and ripped straight out of the wall so how can I even have a chance to call someone to come to help me? Oh, my God! What am I going to do now?

All that I could think of was to just sit down on the couch and not say a word. I just wanted to be very quiet and hope and pray that Terry will calm down and not hurt me anymore.

After an hour of waiting and sitting quietly still on the couch, Terry decides that we both need to go together downstairs to get the maintenance guy to come up and fix the phone

He told me that he did not know what came over him. He did not mean to break the phone. This man is full of the unexpected at any moment of any day, and not in a good way these days. I cannot trust him at all.

Well, Terry goes to the door and pushes the heavy dresser away and put it back into the bedroom where it belongs. He told me that I better not try to leave anywhere without him with me. I told him that I would not. So, we both go downstairs to get the maintenance guy to come up to my apartment and fix the phone and repair the damaged sheetrock on the wall.

After the wall is repaired and the phone was fixed Terry decides to take me to the hospital emergency room to get some x-rays to make sure that I don't have any broken ribs since my chest pains have not gone away yet. We get to the emergency room and get the x-rays done and they show bruising but no broken ribs so I was lucky and very happy that I am going to be alright.

When I was alone with the doctor I tried to tell him why I was having the chest pains and everything that had happened to me but to my surprise he did not even listen to one word that I had said. Instead, whatever lies that Terry had told him about me he believed Terry. After that happened I decided that I was never going to fully trust any doctors at that hospital again. Because why would he believe what Terry had said over me telling the truth? I just could not believe it. I feel as though I am in a big nightmare and it is not going to ever end.

Once we got back to the apartment and ate dinner I had to think fast as Terry decided to take a nap on the couch. I decided that was my chance to escape this madness and this man.

I walked slowly and quietly into the bedroom to grab my purse and the extra set of keys that I had hidden in a tiny box on the top shelf of the closet.

I then tiptoed across the room so as not to make the floorboards creak, praying the whole way that nothing would make a peep. I opened the door slowly, and it made a slight noise. I was surprised that it did not awaken Terry, or even make him stir. So, I dashed out the door as fast as I could and quietly closed the door.

I raced down the back staircase in hopes that no one would see me, especially Terry. Then I ran as fast as I could down the street to the bus stop without ever once looking back and I took the first bus that showed up. It did not matter to me where it would take me at first. Then I thought that if I could only get to the airport I would take the first flight that I could get to get me back to my hometown to my parent's house. That is where I would be safe. I did not care that I did not pack a suitcase because there was no time to stop to do that. I left with whatever was in my purse and the clothes on my back. I just knew that I had to get out of there and as far away as I could as quickly as possible.

Once I got to the airport, I was lucky to find a flight out to Kentucky within an hour. So, I took it. Back then there wasn't extra security, and catching flights was much easier. Once I was on the plane I could finally breathe and began to relax. I cried most of the flight back and eventually drifted off to sleep.

I was back home with my parents in only three hours. I took a cab from the airport and treated it as a surprise visit. I was so ashamed and did not want to alarm everyone even though I'm sure my face was alarming enough. I did not tell my parents what had happened but that I decided to come for a visit. I'm sure they thought there was more to the story, but they never said anything, or asked questions.

My Momma hugged me tight with tears in her eyes, told me she loved me, and was so glad to see me even if it was unexpected.

It was late, so I went up to my old room, and all I wanted was to go to sleep. It was such a long day, and my body hurt. As much as I wanted to get away from this close-minded town, I was glad to be back in my old bed. The next morning, Mom made me breakfast and asked me about New York. After we finished and the kitchen was cleaned up, I told them I needed to take care of a few things. I had my broken eyeglasses inside of my purse so I told my parents that I needed to go and get new ones made while I was in town. I told them I had a fall, and they were broken in the process when they gave me a quizzical look. My Dad offered to take me to the eye doctor's office. I told him thank you and that it would be great.

But before I left to go to get new glasses I called Terry and told him not to hang up the phone and to just listen to me of what I had to say.

I let him know that I did not go to the police yet and that I did not tell anyone about what he had done to me. But that if he is not out of my apartment by the time that I get back in a couple of days that I was going to report him to the police and they will arrest him for kidnapping and assault which will I was pretty sure would ruin his chances of wanting to become a doctor someday.

I told him that he had better get all packed up and out before I get back there and that I meant what I said. I did not even give him a chance to respond and I hung up the phone. I was proud of myself for standing up to him, even if it was only through the phone. I was terrified when I was dialing the number, but God definitely gave me the courage that day to say the right words.

As Dad drove me to the eye doctor's office he had a puzzled look on his face, and took a deep breath before asking me,

"Gloria Ann, is there anything you want to tell me about why you decided that you needed to come home for a visit?"

He caught me a bit off guard, but I kept my composure, and replied, "Dad, there isn't an excuse or real reason other than I was missing my family, and since I didn't have a new eye doctor yet, it would be a good time to come, and kill two birds with one stone. That's really it, Daddy. Besides, we know I can't see well without my glasses!" He chuckled at that, and the subject was dropped.

We went to Dr. Davis to order a new pair of eye glasses for me. Dr. Davis told me that there is no problem in having them mailed to my apartment in New York so I would not have to stay in Kentucky until they were ready if I did not want to. I told him that worked perfectly since I would have to get back to work in New York in a few days.

After spending a couple of days with my family in Kentucky, and my face and body had healed a little more, I decided that I had to go back.

I was ready to go back to New York to face whatever I had to face, even though to be honest, I was completely terrified. But to my surprise when I got back to my apartment building, my car was still parked in my garage space with no damage to it.

With shaky knees, I cautiously went upstairs to my apartment and opened the door with my extra key and carefully looked around my whole place. Probably not the smartest thing to do to go by myself, but I was so ashamed to let anyone know what had really happened. I grabbed a broom to swing if I needed to, and carefully searched every corner of my small apartment.

I was shocked and relieved that Terry was not anywhere to be found inside! Thank you, Jesus! My regular set of keys was setting on top of the dresser in my bedroom. I still planned to see about getting the locks changed, because of course he could have made a set to keep. I didn't put anything past that monster at this point.

Terry had left me a note telling me that he was sorry for everything that had happened and that he promises that he will never hurt me again or ever see me again, if that's really what I want.

Happy tears came running down my face as I read his note. I prayed to God that it was true that Terry had left and will not ever hurt me again.

Chapter 7

Epilogue

As several years went by, I eventually met someone and was married and had two beautiful children. My parents were elated, and I thought I'd found peace. My life was fine until the marriage did not work out. I finally decided that I was worth not being mistreated. I was still happy after some therapy, although I became a single parent. It is not easy being a single mother. We have to do the best that we can because our children need us to help guide them in life, and they don't deserve to be short changed on guidance and love just because the parents can't work it out together.

Sometimes when relationships don't work out it is time to just "Let go and let God," as the saying goes. It is not good to stay in a toxic relationship and especially if the person that you love is not true to you or abusive---that goes for both mental and physical.

After going through many trials and tribulations in life I finally learned how to love myself first and be happy within myself. Because true happiness comes from within. Having a big house, fancy car or no amount of money can make us happy. We have to be happy within ourselves.

Now I know the signs of toxic relationships and I try my best to stay away from those kinds of relationships. It doesn't matter if they are love relationships with a significant other or just friendships. I have learned to not allow anyone to use or abuse me ever again. If I find myself in a situation where I feel taken advantage of or mistreated, I know how to remove myself from it.

I let God lead me to where I need to be and to whom that I need to be with. Each day is a gift that you wake up and a chance for a new start. Our God is a God of grace and forgiveness. We all fall short, but each day is a new chance. If I forgive the ones who have hurt me (and I have, even Terry), I can be free to be me and live my life to the fullest! Through faith in God we can get through anything!

I live by what I personally call God's promise as The Spirit of Sixteen. It is the King James Version of the Holy Bible in the book of John chapter 3 verse 16. This Bible verse helped me to stay strong throughout my life, and has been used in various parts of the story:

For God so loved the world that he gave his only begotten son that whosoever believeth in him should not parish but have everlasting life.

Here are some signs that you are in a toxic relationship.

If the person is/has:

1. Too jealous-they don't like anyone paying attention to you
2. Non-trusting
3. Cheats on you
4. Have extreme anger problems
5. Does not allow you to see or talk to your family or friends
6. Does not want to meet any of your friends or family
7. Disrespects or abuses you in any way
8. Does not allow you to go anywhere without them
9. Does not want you to talk on the phone
10. Only likes to text you

11. Always goes through your phone to see who you have been talking to
12. Always tear you down instead of trying to help build you up…aka condescending
13. Does not care about what you want
14. Doesn't allow you to be yourself
15. Hard to communicate

Love & Light with Poems/Songs/Spoken Word
Chapter 8

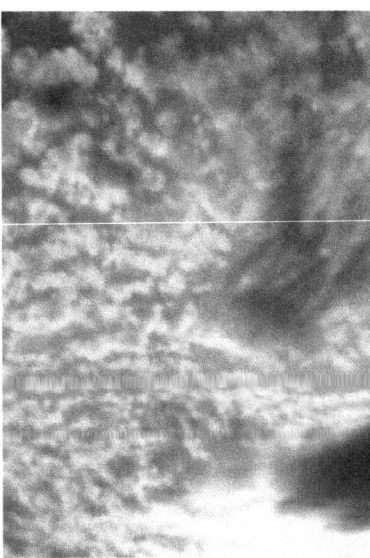

We are born in this world pure without any flaws like the beautiful blue sky.

But as we grow up and go through this journey of life there may be many trials or tribulations. So our beautiful blue sky can turn into dark murky clouds as the hurt and pain may come our way.

At the end of our journey we can always remember even though there may be darkness there is always the light at the end of the tunnel.

©2022 M. Ann Machen Pritchard

I believe that once we are healed from our hurt and pain of life that we can find true love. Or that true love will find us.

My Happy Place
By
M. Ann Machen Pritchard

I'm in my happy place
Seeing you face to face
Sitting with you on this swing
I know you are my everything

I have found my true love
Sent to me from above
With God's Grace
I'm in my happy place

© M. Ann Machen Pritchard 2022

Song: "TONIGHT"

INTRO

(SPOKEN) BABY... TONIGHT, I'M GONNA LOVE YOU LIKE YOU'VE NEVER BEEN LOVED BEFORE.

VERSE: I'LL SHOW YOU I AM THE BEST

I'LL MAKE YOU FORGET THE REST

YOU'LL HAVE NO LESS...

I WILL MAKE YOU SCREAM AND SHOUT

THEN YOU'LL KNOW WHAT LOVE'S ABOUT

I HAVE NO DOUBT

I'LL HOLD YOU CLOSE TO ME

CHORUS: TONIGHT, IS OUR NIGHT

AND I KNOW OUR LOVE IS RIGHT

TONIGHT

(BRIDGE) VERSE: YOU AND I ARE ONE TOGETHER

AND OUR LOVE WILL LAST FOREVER

AND EVER

I'M SO GLAD THAT YOU ARE MINE

I'LL LOVE YOU TIL THE END OF TIME

BABY YOU'RE SO FINE

I'LL HOLD YOU CLOSE TO ME

CHORUS: TONIGHT, IS OUR NIGHT

AND I KNOW OUR LOVE IS RIGHT

TONIGHT BABY

(BRIDGE) CHANGE: (SPOKEN)

YOU SHOULD KNOW MY LOVE IS REAL...

THE WAY I SHOW YOU HOW I FEEL

I LOVE TO HOLD YOU IN MY ARMS

YOU THRILL ME WITH YOUR CHARMS

I'LL MAKE ALL OF YOUR DREAMS COME TRUE

I'LL SHOW YOU HOW MUCH I LOVE YOU

THIS IS OUR NIGHT

TONIGHT

©1992 ANN MACHEN PRITCHARD ALL RIGHTS RESERVED

With Faith in God we can get through anything!

I don't have to trick my body to be a hottie!

Written by M. Ann Machen Pritchard © 2022

I don't have to trick my body to be a hottie.

No matter my size I'm a hottie in his eyes.

I don't have to trick my body to be a hottie.

No matter my size I'm a hottie in his eyes.

He loves me from my head to my toes

Everybody knows.

And I don't mind.

Because he's all mine.

I'm very unique.

I'm who he will seek.

He wants to be mine

Because I'm one of a kind.

You're the kind of man that I have been waiting for.

Written by M. Ann Machen Pritchard ©2013

You're the kind of man that I have been waiting for.

Yes, you're the kind of man that I have been looking for.

A man who understands me.

A man who lets me be me!

A man who loves me unconditionally!

When the Sunlight Kisses My Face

Written by M. Ann Machen Pritchard ©2014

When the sunlight kisses my face.

I long for your embrace.

To hold you close to me.

With you I feel free.

Where are you?

I know you love me, too!

I know you are out here somewhere my dear.

I will keep waiting until you are here.

When the sunlight kisses my face

I long for your embrace.

Final Thoughts

Are you Happy? If so, good for you! If you are not then remember that happiness comes from within and there is nothing and no one that can make you happy truly but yourself. Only you can change your life if you want things to change. So live your life to the fullest and be happy! Keep smiling and laughing and be the best that you can be because you are just fine. Don't ever let anyone say that you cannot make your dreams come true. Follow your dreams and your heart and you can make it happen!

Always remember that life is a struggle at times. We all go through good times, bad times, rough times, sad times, and happy times. But know that it is not the end of the world when things don't always go our way! It is ok to cry and let our feelings out because we have to release the stresses in our lives. Then get those smiles and laughs back and know that we will be okay. Learn to forgive those who hurt us and live life to the fullest. Happiness and love in our life begins with us! Keep smiling and laughing and you can feel better! We all have been through so many trials and tribulations but we cannot let our ups and downs destroy us. We must keep on living and loving life!

Always remember that someone out there does Love you! Don't feel down and out. Keep smiling and believe that you are somebody and success does not mean how rich you are financially. Learn to Love yourself positively then you will be able to Love someone else. Don't hate, be angry or be a Narcissist. Be loving, kind, caring, and respectful of yourself and of others so your life will be better in the long run.

Keep smiling and laughing and don't be afraid to tell someone that you trust if you are hurting about something that is heavy on your mind! It is best to talk about it and ask for help so you can release the stress that is bottled up inside of you! Don't let it carry on for the rest of your life and make you miserable. Talk about it and get the help that you need so you can live a better life and be happy both inside and out! Learn that it is ok to seek help with anything that you want or need to talk about and learn to live life to the fullest! Life is too short to not be happy. No money, no big house or new car will make you happy fully. You have to deal with the real that you are bottling up inside your mind and heart! Talk about it and release it so you can be free of the stress and pain in your life. Release it so you can be free to be you! Sending hugs and prayers to all.

Remember this if you don't remember anything else that I have ever said:

Hate feeds on Hate!

Love feeds on Love!

Anger feeds on Anger!

Prejudice feeds on Prejudice!
War feeds on War!
Balance in life feeds on Balance in life!
Happiness feeds on Happiness!
Injustice feeds on Injustice!
Education feeds on Education!
Forgiveness feeds on Forgiveness!

Let's all work together to make this world a better place for all! No matter how rich or poor we are.

Hey, to all of the men out here who don't know how to love one woman to be loyal only to her and not cheat on her...women age and you yourself age and you should not expect your mate to still look like she is 25 when she is older. And I must say, yes you don't still look 25 years old either! So why do you want to continue to put us beautiful women down and don't think that you may have some flaws in your looks or life either? No one is perfect out here but God! Something to think about. We are ourselves and we love being ourselves and we love our children to the universe and back unconditionally. So why can you not love us back when we love you?

Make it a great day! Smile more and laugh more and it can make you feel better! Believe me, I go through many trials and tribulations in my own life and if I did not smile and laugh more I would be a basket case every single day. I have learned through the years that our lives may not go the way that we planned or would like it to but we can pick ourselves up and not let things keep us down too long. If we focus only on the bad times or sad times then we don't give ourselves a chance to be happy and live our lives to the fullest!

I am very thankful for all of my friends and family who really care and support me and not take advantage of my kindness. I pray for the ones who laughed at me and told me that I can never do anything or that I am not good enough! I pray for the ones who took advantage of my kindness to help them but they stole from me instead of being thankful for me helping them. Well, I am good enough to be what ever I want to be in life and I have accomplished many things that I ever dreamed of doing and I am not stopping or giving up. I know my purpose in life and I am living my purpose that God put me on this earth to do.

Fly High in the Sky

By M. Ann Machen Pritchard

Fly high in the sky.

I did not want you to die.

But I guess it was time for you to part from us.

So I will not cry or make a big fuss.

Because that is not what you would want me to do from the start.

You would want me to remember that you still live on inside of my heart.

Fly high in the sky.

I did not want you to die.

I will always love you and treasure your memories.

Now rest my dear loved one into the new centuries.

©2020 M. Ann Machen Pritchard

A Brand New Day
Written by M. Ann Machen Pritchard

I want to be loved.
I want to feel that I'm loved.
I want to feel that I'm respected and not rejected.
I don't want to be abused, beaten and used.
No more I say...
I'm going to make this a brand new day!

I want to feel loved.
I want to be pure as a lily white dove.
I'm strong...
It's not my fault.
I've done no wrong...
I cannot forget what you have done.
But I can forgive you as I sit here in the morning sun!

© M. Ann Machen Pritchard 2013

A NEW LIFE

Words and Music by:
M. Ann Machen Pritchard

Once upon a time all I had was doubt Once upon a time
I thought I had no way out But Jesus came my way and gave me a brand new day and a new

1. Chorus
life A new life He washed and cleansed my soul & now my life's pure gold I have a new life
A new life Once upon a time all I knew was sin Once upon a time
I thought I had no friend But Jesus came my way and gave me a brand new day and a new

2. Chorus
life A new life Just put your life in his hands & let him guide you through
his plans He will take good care of you & make your life brand new

©2013 M. Ann Machen Pritchard
All Rights Reserved

Other books by M. Ann Machen Pritchard:

Phil the Pill and Friends Making Positive Choices

Val's World Featuring The Family Unity Roundtable

Thank you in advance for visiting our website at:

www.mampcreations.com

Other music:

Drugs and Alcohol by MAMP Creations

About the Author:

M. Ann Pritchard aka M. Ann (Machen) Pritchard, aka Ann Pritchard is the Author/Illustrator/Songwriter of the children's books, Phil the Pill and Friends Making Positive Choices and Val's World Featuring The Family Unity Roundtable. Also, the songwriter of the song 'Drugs and Alcohol by MAMP Creations. The books were written to help encourage children to stay in school to get their education, learn how to read and make positive choices. They also teach children positive communication skills and help bring families closer together. Her book, The Spirit of Sixteen, is based on a true story.

Her passion and mission is to encourage everyone that it is not the end of the world when things don't always go our way. She strongly believes that if we get a good education and learn to make positive choices at an early age, we can get through more difficult challenges now and later in life.

Ann has appeared on several Radio and TV Shows including, Fox 9 Morning News, The Art Cunningham Show, Lovepower, Crossroads, Let's Learn to Get Along, Motivation with Ron Henderson, the Fitness King, WBEJ 107.9 FM and 1240 AM, KNOF 95.3 FM, KMTL760AM, the 3-minute egg dot com, Authors First, the ChildrenAuthorShow dot com and In and Out Of Sports Show for Authors Night with Coach Butch McAdams. Also, in newspapers including, The Maywood Herald, Elizabethton Star, Johnson City Press, Spokesman-Recorder, The African News Journal and Insight News. Ann was also interviewed in the Voyage Minnesota Magazine. She is available to speak at schools, libraries, on Radio and TV shows or any events involving the community for positive interventions. The books were nominated in the MN Book Awards and Hollywood Book Awards. Her books have been received positively by many, including Hillary Rodham Clinton, Laura Bush and Sarah Ferguson, Duchess of York.

Ann is a former Sales Representative specializing in the Advertising Specialty, Apparel, and Banner/Sign Industry. She received a Lifetime Achievement Award in Quality Excellence for 99.9% Accuracy from Trimark presented by Rivers' End Trading Company. She received a Service Award from the Plymouth Avenue Art Studio in Minneapolis, MN. Ann is a Winner in 50 Great Writers You Should Be Reading, 2013-14 Edition. She is from a family of 16 children in which they had a Gospel Singing Group, 'The Machen Spirituals' who sang on Radio and TV in her childhood days. In her hometown area of East Tennessee, she is a former, Model, Actress, Singer and Make-up Artist. She has been in productions at the Des Moines Playhouse, in Des Moines, IA under direction of Ted Kehoe, Outdoor dramas such as 'The Wataugan's' presently known as 'Liberty', Nils Cruz, Director and 'The Lost State: A Frontier Chronicle', C. Warren Robertson, Director in East Tennessee. Also, she has been in commercials for Tennessee Tourism and was in the Minneapolis the Movie test trailer, Peter Kelley, Director. Ann plays the role of Grandma in, 'The Christmas You Don't Know', Amber Patton and Christine Clayburg Award Winning Directors. She plays the role of Lila in, 'The Wrath of

Grapes', Amber Patton, Director and the role of Grandma in Enigma Lake, Jared Elkin, Director. She is the Line Producer for 'Enigma Lake.' She also appeared in 'Body Not Included, Veronica Wayne, Director and 'Safe at Home', Maya Montague, Director. She is proud to be the sister of 5 Military Veterans. Ann is the owner of an online Retail Store, MAMP Creations that sells merchandise with positive messages to help change the world. She is so proud that MAMP Creations is listed in the Gift/Promotional Items section of the Super Bowl LII Business Connect Program Resource Guide. www.mampcreations.com. Ann has also volunteered for communities and organizations throughout the years.

www.ingramcontent.com/pod-product-compliance
Lightning Source LLC
Chambersburg PA
CBHW060524100426
42743CB00009B/1427